YO-AFX-493

Recipes to Share

BAKE SALE

Publications International, Ltd.

Favorite Brand Name Recipes at www.fbnr.com

Pictured on the front cover *(top to bottom):* Turtle Brownies *(page 46)* and Chocolate Syrup Swirl Cake *(page 70).*
Pictured on the back cover: Spiced Orange Cranberry Muffins *(page 4).*

ISBN-13: 978-1-4127-9797-9
ISBN-10: 1-4127-9797-7

Library of Congress Control Number: 2009920139

Manufactured in China.

8 7 6 5 4 3 2 1

Microwave Cooking: Microwave ovens vary in wattage. Use the cooking times as guidelines and check for doneness before adding more time.

Preparation/Cooking Times: Preparation times are based on the approximate amount of time required to assemble the recipe before cooking, baking, chilling or serving. These times include preparation steps such as measuring, chopping and mixing. The fact that some preparations and cooking can be done simultaneously is taken into account. Preparation of optional ingredients and serving suggestions is not included.

Table of
CONTENTS

Muffin MADNESS

Spiced Orange Cranberry Muffins

½ cup dried cranberries
3 tablespoons packed brown sugar
1 cup orange juice
1 egg white
2 tablespoons canola or vegetable oil
1 cup whole wheat flour
½ cup all-purpose flour
1½ teaspoons baking powder
½ teaspoon ground cinnamon
¼ teaspoon ground nutmeg

1. Preheat oven to 400°F. Grease 8 standard (2½-inch) muffin cups or line with paper baking cups. Combine cranberries and brown sugar in small bowl. Stir in orange juice, egg white and oil; let stand 5 minutes.

2. Combine whole wheat flour, all-purpose flour, baking powder, cinnamon and nutmeg in medium bowl. Add cranberry mixture to flour mixture; stir just until combined. Spoon batter into prepared muffin cups, filling three-fourths full.

3. Bake 18 to 20 minutes or until toothpick inserted into centers comes out clean. Immediately remove from pan; cool completely on wire rack. *Makes 8 muffins*

Blueberry Cinnamon Muffins

1¼ cups all-purpose flour
½ cup CREAM OF WHEAT® Cinnamon Swirl Instant Hot Cereal, uncooked
½ cup sugar, divided
1 tablespoon baking powder
2 teaspoons ground cinnamon
½ teaspoon salt
1 cup fat-free milk
1 egg
2 tablespoons oil
1 teaspoon vanilla extract
1 cup fresh or frozen blueberries
2 tablespoons apple juice

1. Preheat oven to 400°F. Grease 12 (2½-inch) muffin cups. Mix flour, Cream of Wheat, ¼ cup sugar, baking powder, cinnamon and salt in medium bowl; set aside.

2. Beat milk, egg, oil and vanilla with wire whisk in separate bowl until well blended. Add to dry ingredients; stir just until moistened. Gently stir in blueberries. Spoon evenly into prepared muffin cups, filling each cup two-thirds full.

3. Bake 18 to 20 minutes or until toothpick inserted into centers comes out clean. Remove muffins from pan.

4. Brush tops of warm muffins with apple juice; roll in remaining ¼ cup sugar. Serve warm.   *Makes 12 muffins*

Tip: To make Strawberries 'n Cream Muffins, use CREAM OF WHEAT® Strawberries 'n Cream Instant Hot Cereal and frozen strawberries.

Piña Colada Muffins

2 cups all-purpose flour
¾ cup sugar
½ cup flaked coconut
2 teaspoons baking powder
½ teaspoon baking soda
½ teaspoon salt
2 eggs
1 cup sour cream
1 can (8 ounces) crushed pineapple in juice, undrained
¼ cup (½ stick) butter, melted
⅛ teaspoon coconut extract
    Additional flaked coconut (optional)

1. Preheat oven to 400°F. Spray 18 standard (2½-inch) muffin cups with nonstick cooking spray or line with paper baking cups.

2. Combine flour, sugar, coconut, baking powder, baking soda and salt in large bowl; mix well.

3. Beat eggs in medium bowl with electric mixer at medium speed 1 to 2 minutes or until frothy. Beat in sour cream, pineapple with juice, butter and coconut extract. Add to flour mixture; beat just until combined. Spoon batter into prepared muffin cups, filling three-fourths full.

4. Bake 15 to 20 minutes or until toothpick inserted into centers comes out clean. If desired, sprinkle tops of muffins with additional coconut after first 10 minutes. Cool in pans 2 minutes. Remove to wire racks; cool completely.   *Makes 18 muffins*

Ginger Squash Muffins

1½ cups all-purpose flour
⅓ cup whole wheat flour
⅓ cup granulated sugar
¼ cup packed dark brown sugar
2½ teaspoons baking powder
1 teaspoon ground cinnamon
½ teaspoon baking soda
½ teaspoon salt
½ teaspoon ground ginger
1 cup frozen winter squash,* thawed
2 eggs, beaten
⅓ cup canola oil
¼ cup finely chopped walnuts
2 tablespoons finely chopped crystallized ginger (optional)

One 12-ounce package frozen squash yields about 1 cup squash.

1. Preheat oven to 375°F. Spray 12 standard (2½-inch) muffin cups with nonstick cooking spray.

2. Combine all-purpose flour, whole wheat flour, granulated sugar, brown sugar, baking powder, cinnamon, baking soda, salt and ground ginger in large bowl; mix well.

3. Combine squash, eggs and oil in small bowl. Add to flour mixture; stir just until blended. (Do not beat.) Stir in walnuts and crystallized ginger, if desired. Spoon batter into prepared muffin cups, filling two-thirds full.

4. Bake 18 to 20 minutes or until toothpick inserted into centers comes out clean. Cool in pan 5 minutes. Remove to wire rack; cool completely.   *Makes 12 muffins*

Banana Peanut Butter Chip Muffins

2 cups all-purpose flour
¾ cup sugar
2 teaspoons baking powder
½ teaspoon baking soda
¼ teaspoon salt
1 cup mashed ripe bananas (about 2 large)
½ cup (1 stick) butter, melted
2 eggs, beaten
⅓ cup buttermilk
1½ teaspoons vanilla
1 cup peanut butter chips
½ cup chopped peanuts

1. Preheat oven to 375°F. Grease 15 standard (2½-inch) muffins cups or line with paper baking cups.

2. Combine flour, sugar, baking powder, baking soda and salt in large bowl. Whisk bananas, butter, eggs, buttermilk and vanilla in medium bowl until well blended.

3. Add banana mixture to flour mixture; stir just until blended. Gently fold in peanut butter chips. Spoon batter into prepared muffin cups, filling three-fourths full. Sprinkle with chopped peanuts.

4. Bake 20 minutes or until toothpick inserted into centers comes out clean. Cool in pans 2 minutes. Remove to wire racks; cool completely.   *Makes 15 muffins*

Tip: Substitute a mixture of chocolate chips and peanut butter chips for the peanut butter chips for a combination of three great flavors in one muffin.

Toffee Crunch Muffins

1½ cups all-purpose flour
⅓ cup packed brown sugar
2 teaspoons baking powder
½ teaspoon baking soda
½ teaspoon salt
½ cup milk
½ cup sour cream
1 egg, beaten
3 tablespoons butter, melted
1 teaspoon vanilla
3 bars (1.4 ounces each) chocolate-covered toffee, chopped, divided

1. Preheat oven to 400°F. Grease 36 mini (1¾-inch) muffin cups or line with paper baking cups.

2. Combine flour, brown sugar, baking powder, baking soda and salt in large bowl. Combine milk, sour cream, egg, butter and vanilla in small bowl until well blended. Stir into flour mixture just until moistened. Fold in two thirds of toffee. Spoon batter into prepared muffin cups, filling almost full. Sprinkle evenly with remaining toffee.

3. Bake 16 to 18 minutes or until toothpick inserted into centers comes out clean. Cool in pans 2 minutes. Remove to wire racks; cool completely.

Makes 36 mini muffins

Variation: For larger muffins, spoon batter into 10 standard (2½-inch) greased or paper-lined muffin cups. Bake at 350°F 20 minutes or until toothpick inserted into centers comes out clean. Makes 10 muffins.

Apple-Cheddar Muffins

1 cup whole wheat flour
1 cup all-purpose flour
2 tablespoons sugar
1 tablespoon baking powder
½ teaspoon salt
1 cup peeled, chopped apple
1 cup grated CABOT® Mild or Sharp Cheddar
2 eggs
1 cup milk
4 tablespoons CABOT® Salted Butter, melted

1. Preheat oven to 400°F. Butter 12 muffin cups or coat with nonstick cooking spray.

2. In mixing bowl, stir together whole wheat and white flour, sugar, baking powder and salt. Add apples and cheese and toss to combine.

3. In another bowl, whisk eggs lightly. Whisk in milk and butter. Make well in center of dry ingredients; add milk mixture and gently stir in dry ingredients from side until just combined.

4. Divide batter among prepared muffin cups. Bake for 20 minutes, or until muffins feel firm when lightly pressed on top. *Makes 12 muffins*

Chocolate Chip Muffins

1¾ cups all-purpose flour
⅓ cup packed brown sugar
2 tablespoons unsweetened cocoa powder
2½ teaspoons baking powder
1½ teaspoons ground cinnamon
¼ teaspoon salt
1 cup milk
1 egg, lightly beaten
¼ cup unsweetened applesauce
2 tablespoons butter, melted
1 teaspoon vanilla
⅔ cup mini semisweet chocolate chips

1. Preheat oven to 400°F. Spray 12 standard (2½-inch) muffin cups with nonstick cooking spray or line with foil baking cups.

2. Combine flour, brown sugar, cocoa, baking powder, cinnamon and salt in medium bowl. Stir together milk, egg, applesauce, butter and vanilla in small bowl until blended. Add to flour mixture; stir just until blended. Fold in chocolate chips. Spoon batter evenly into prepared muffin cups.

3. Bake 13 to 15 minutes or until toothpick inserted into centers comes out clean. Cool in pan 5 minutes. Remove to wire rack; cool completely.   *Makes 12 muffins*

Maple Magic Muffins

½ cup plus 3 tablespoons maple syrup,* divided
¼ cup chopped walnuts
2 tablespoons butter, melted
2 cups all-purpose flour
¾ cup sugar
2 teaspoons baking powder
½ teaspoon baking soda
½ teaspoon salt
¼ teaspoon ground cinnamon
¾ cup plus 1 tablespoon milk
½ cup vegetable oil
1 egg
½ teaspoon vanilla

For best flavor and texture, use pure maple syrup, not pancake syrup.

1. Preheat oven to 400°F. Grease 12 standard (2½-inch) nonstick muffin cups. Place 2 teaspoons maple syrup, 1 teaspoon walnuts and ½ teaspoon melted butter in each cup.

2. Combine flour, sugar, baking powder, baking soda, salt and cinnamon in large bowl; mix well.

3. Whisk milk, oil, egg, remaining 3 tablespoons maple syrup and vanilla in medium bowl until well blended. Add to flour mixture; stir just until blended. Spoon batter into prepared muffin cups, filling two-thirds full. Place muffin pan on baking sheet to catch any drips (maple syrup may overflow slightly).

4. Bake 20 to 25 minutes or until toothpick inserted into centers comes out clean. Invert pan onto wire rack covered with waxed paper. Cool muffins slightly; serve warm.   *Makes 12 muffins*

Orange-Raisin Bran Muffins

MAZOLA PURE® Cooking Spray
⅓ cup boiling water
1 cup natural high-fiber bran cereal shreds
½ cup orange juice
1 egg
½ cup KARO® Light or Dark Corn Syrup
¼ cup sugar
¼ cup MAZOLA® Oil
½ cup raisins
1 cup flour
1 teaspoon baking soda
¼ teaspoon salt

1. Preheat oven to 400°F. Spray 12 (2½-inch) muffin pan cups with cooking spray. In large bowl pour boiling water over cereal; let stand 2 minutes. Stir in orange juice, egg, corn syrup, sugar, oil and raisins.

2. In medium bowl combine flour, baking soda and salt; set aside. Stir flour mixture into cereal mixture until well blended. Spoon into prepared muffin pan cups.

3. Bake 15 to 20 minutes or until lightly browned and firm to touch. Cool in pan on wire rack 5 minutes; remove from pan. *Makes 12 muffins*

Sweet Potato Muffins

2 cups all-purpose flour
¾ cup chopped walnuts
¾ cup golden raisins
½ cup packed brown sugar
1 tablespoon baking powder
1 teaspoon ground cinnamon
½ teaspoon salt
½ teaspoon baking soda
¼ teaspoon ground nutmeg
1 cup mashed cooked sweet potato
¾ cup milk
½ cup (1 stick) butter, melted
2 eggs, beaten
1½ teaspoons vanilla

1. Preheat oven to 400°F. Grease 24 standard (2½-inch) muffin cups.

2. Combine flour, walnuts, raisins, brown sugar, baking powder, cinnamon, salt, baking soda and nutmeg in medium bowl; stir until well blended.

3. Combine sweet potato, milk, butter, eggs and vanilla in large bowl; stir until well blended. Add flour mixture to sweet potato mixture; stir just until dry ingredients are moistened. Spoon batter evenly into prepared muffin cups.

4. Bake 15 minutes or until toothpick inserted into centers comes out clean. Cool in pans 5 minutes. Remove to wire racks; cool completely.   *Makes 24 muffins*

Pineapple Carrot Raisin Muffins

   2 cups all-purpose flour
   1 cup sugar
1½ teaspoons baking powder
   1 teaspoon ground cinnamon
   1 can (8 ounces) DOLE® Crushed Pineapple, undrained
   2 eggs
   ½ cup (1 stick) butter or margarine, melted
   1 cup DOLE® Seedless or Golden Raisins
   ½ cup shredded DOLE® Carrots

- Combine flour, sugar, baking powder and cinnamon in large bowl.
- Add undrained pineapple, eggs, butter, raisins and carrots; stir just until blended.
- Spoon evenly into 36 mini-muffin cups sprayed with nonstick vegetable cooking spray.
- Bake at 375°F., 15 to 20 minutes or until toothpick inserted in center comes out clean. Remove muffins from pans onto wire rack to cool.

Makes 3 dozen mini-muffins

For 2½-inch Muffins: Spoon batter into 2½-inch muffin pans instead of mini-muffin pans. Bake as directed for 20 to 25 minutes. Cool as directed.

Best Ever
BARS

Gooey Caramel Chocolate Bars

2 cups all-purpose flour
1 cup granulated sugar
¼ teaspoon salt
2 cups (4 sticks) butter, divided
1 cup packed light brown sugar
⅓ cup light corn syrup
1 cup (6 ounces) semisweet chocolate chips

1. Preheat oven to 350°F. Line 13×9-inch baking pan with foil. Combine flour, granulated sugar and salt in medium bowl. Cut in 14 tablespoons (1¾ sticks) butter until mixture resembles coarse crumbs. Press onto bottom of prepared pan.

2. Bake 18 to 20 minutes or until lightly browned around edges. Cool completely in pan on wire rack.

3. Combine 1 cup (2 sticks) butter, brown sugar and corn syrup in medium heavy saucepan. Cook over medium heat 5 to 8 minutes or until mixture boils, stirring frequently. Boil gently 2 minutes without stirring. Immediately pour over cooled base; spread evenly to edges of pan. Cool completely.

4. Melt chocolate and remaining 2 tablespoons butter in double boiler over simmering water. Pour over caramel layer; spread evenly to edges of pan. Refrigerate 10 minutes or until chocolate begins to set. Cool completely at room temperature. Remove foil; cut into bars.   *Makes 3 dozen bars*

Apricot Shortbread Diamonds

1 package (about 18 ounces) yellow cake mix
2 eggs
¼ cup vegetable oil
1 tablespoon water
1 cup apricot jam or orange marmalade
1 cup diced dried apricots (about 6 ounces)
1 cup sliced almonds

1. Preheat oven to 350°F. Line 15×10-inch jelly-roll pan with foil and spray lightly with nonstick cooking spray.

2. Beat cake mix, eggs, oil and water in large bowl with electric mixer at medium speed until well blended. With damp hands, press dough into prepared pan.

3. Place jam in small microwavable bowl. Heat on HIGH 20 seconds to soften. Spread jam evenly over dough; sprinkle apricots and almonds over top.

4. Bake 25 minutes or until edges are browned and jam bubbles at edges. Cool completely in pan on wire rack. Remove foil; cut into diamond-shaped bars.

Makes about 2 dozen bars

APRICOT SHORTBREAD DIAMONDS

Butterscotch Toffee Gingersnap Squares

40 gingersnap cookies
⅓ cup butter, melted
1 can (14 ounces) sweetened condensed milk
1½ teaspoons vanilla
1 cup butterscotch chips
½ cup pecan pieces
½ cup chopped peanuts
½ cup milk chocolate toffee bits
½ cup mini semisweet chocolate chips

1. Preheat oven to 350°F. Line 13×9-inch baking pan with foil, leaving 1-inch overhang. Spray foil with nonstick cooking spray.

2. Place cookies in food processor; process until crumbs form. Combine 2 cups crumbs and butter in medium bowl; mix well. Press crumb mixture evenly into bottom of prepared pan. Bake 4 to 5 minutes or until light brown around edges.

3. Combine condensed milk and vanilla in small bowl; pour over warm crust. Sprinkle with butterscotch chips, pecans, peanuts, toffee bits and chocolate chips. Press down gently.

4. Bake 15 to 18 minutes or until bubbly and golden. Cool completely in pan on wire rack. Remove foil; cut into bars. Store in airtight container.

Makes 3 dozen bars

O'Henrietta Bars

MAZOLA PURE® Cooking Spray
½ cup (1 stick) butter or margarine, softened
½ cup packed brown sugar
½ cup KARO® Light or Dark Corn Syrup
1 teaspoon vanilla
3 cups quick oats, uncooked
½ cup (3 ounces) semi-sweet chocolate chips
¼ cup creamy peanut butter

1. Preheat oven to 350°F. Spray 8- or 9-inch square baking pan with cooking spray.

2. Beat butter, brown sugar, corn syrup and vanilla in large bowl with mixer at medium speed until smooth. Stir in oats. Press into prepared pan.

3. Bake 25 minutes or until center is barely firm. Cool on wire rack 5 minutes.

4. Sprinkle with chocolate chips; top with small spoonfuls of peanut butter. Let stand 5 minutes; spread peanut butter and chocolate over bars, swirling to marble.

5. Cool completely on wire rack before cutting. Cut into bars; refrigerate 15 minutes to set topping.   *Makes 24 bars*

Cinnamon Apple Pie Bars

1 package (about 18 ounces) spice cake mix with pudding in the mix
2 cups uncooked old-fashioned oats
½ teaspoon ground cinnamon
¾ cup (1½ sticks) cold butter, cut into pieces
1 egg
1 can (21 ounces) apple pie filling and topping

1. Preheat oven to 350°F. Spray 13×9-inch baking pan with nonstick cooking spray.

2. Combine cake mix, oats and cinnamon in large bowl. Cut in butter using pastry blender or fingers until butter is evenly distributed and no large pieces remain (mixture will be dry and have clumps). Stir in egg until well mixed.

3. With damp hands, press about three-fourths oat mixture into bottom of prepared pan. Spread apple pie filling evenly over top. Crumble remaining oat mixture over filling. Bake 25 to 30 minutes or until top and edges are lightly browned. Cool completely in pan on wire rack. Cut into bars.   *Makes about 2 dozen bars*

PB&J Cookie Bars

1 package (about 18 ounces) yellow cake mix with pudding in the mix
1 cup peanut butter
½ cup vegetable oil
2 eggs
1 cup strawberry jam
1 cup peanut butter chips

1. Preheat oven to 350°F. Line 15×10-inch jelly-roll pan with foil and spray lightly with nonstick cooking spray.

2. Beat cake mix, peanut butter, oil and eggs in large bowl with electric mixer at medium speed until well blended. With damp hands, press mixture evenly into prepared pan. Bake 20 minutes.

3. Meanwhile, place jam in small microwavable bowl; heat on HIGH 20 seconds to soften. Spread jam evenly over cookie base. Scatter peanut butter chips over top.

4. Bake 10 minutes or until edges are browned. Cool completely in pan on wire rack. Remove foil; cut into bars.   *Makes about 3 dozen bars*

Black Forest Bars

1 package (about 18 ounces) dark chocolate cake mix
½ cup (1 stick) unsalted butter, melted
1 egg
½ teaspoon almond extract
1¼ cup sliced almonds, divided
1 jar (about 16 ounces) maraschino cherries, well drained
½ cup semisweet chocolate chips

1. Preheat oven to 350°F. Line 13×9-inch baking pan with foil.

2. Beat cake mix, butter, egg and almond extract in large bowl with electric mixer at medium speed. Stir in ¾ cup almonds.

3. Press dough into bottom of prepared pan. Top evenly with cherries. Bake 20 to 25 minutes or until toothpick inserted into center comes out clean. Cool completely in pan on wire rack.

4. Place chocolate chips in small resealable food storage bag; seal bag. Microwave on HIGH 1 to 1½ minutes, kneading bag every 30 seconds until melted and smooth. Cut tiny corner from bag; drizzle chocolate over top. Sprinkle with remaining ½ cup almonds. Remove foil; cut into bars.   *Makes about 2 dozen bars*

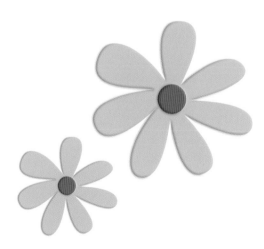

Taffy Apple Bars

1 package (18 ounces) refrigerated sugar cookie dough
1 package (18 ounces) refrigerated peanut butter cookie dough
½ cup all-purpose flour
3½ to 4 cups chopped cored peeled apples (about 2 large)
1 cup chopped peanuts
½ cup caramel ice cream topping

1. Preheat oven to 350°F. Lightly grease 13×9-inch baking pan. Let doughs stand at room temperature 15 minutes.

2. Beat doughs and flour in large bowl with electric mixer at medium speed until well blended. Press dough into bottom of prepared pan. Layer apples evenly over dough; press down lightly. Sprinkle with peanuts.

3. Bake 35 minutes or until edges are browned and center is firm to the touch. Cool completely in pan on wire rack. Drizzle with caramel topping. Cut into bars.

Makes about 2 dozen bars

Gingerbread Cheesecake Bars

1 package (8 ounces) cream cheese, softened
⅔ cup sugar, divided
3 eggs
1½ teaspoons ground ginger, divided
½ teaspoon vanilla
½ cup (1 stick) butter, softened
¾ cup molasses
2 cups all-purpose flour
1 teaspoon baking soda
¾ teaspoon ground cinnamon
¼ teaspoon salt
¼ teaspoon ground allspice

1. Preheat oven to 350°F. Grease 13×9-inch baking pan.

2. Beat cream cheese and ⅓ cup sugar in medium bowl with electric mixer at medium speed until light and fluffy. Add 1 egg, ½ teaspoon ginger and vanilla; beat until well blended and smooth. Refrigerate until ready to use.

3. Beat butter and remaining ⅓ cup sugar in large bowl at medium speed until light and fluffy. Add molasses and remaining 2 eggs; beat until well blended. Combine flour, baking soda, remaining 1 teaspoon ginger, cinnamon, salt and allspice in medium bowl. Add flour mixture to butter mixture; beat just until blended. Spread batter evenly in prepared pan. Drop cream cheese mixture by spoonfuls onto gingerbread batter; swirl into batter with knife.

4. Bake 25 to 30 minutes or until toothpick inserted into center comes out clean. Cool completely in pan on wire rack. Cut into bars.   *Makes 2 dozen bars*

Chocolate Oatmeal Caramel Bars

1¼ cups uncooked old-fashioned oats
1 cup all-purpose flour
½ cup plus 2 tablespoons packed brown sugar, divided
2 tablespoons unsweetened Dutch process cocoa powder*
¾ cup (1½ sticks) butter, melted
1 can (14 ounces) sweetened condensed milk
⅓ cup butter
½ cup chopped pecans

While Dutch process cocoa powder has a stronger flavor and will bake a darker color, natural unsweetened cocoa powder may be substituted.

1. Preheat oven to 350°F. Combine oats, flour, ½ cup brown sugar and cocoa in medium bowl. Add ¾ cup melted butter; mix until crumbly. Reserve 1 cup oat mixture for topping; press remaining oat mixture into bottom of ungreased 8-inch square baking pan. Bake 15 minutes.

2. Meanwhile, combine condensed milk, ⅓ cup butter and remaining 2 tablespoons brown sugar in medium saucepan; cook and stir over medium heat 10 minutes or until thick and pale brown in color.

3. Cool milk mixture slightly until thickened; spread evenly over baked crust. Let stand 5 minutes or until set. Add pecans to reserved oat mixture; sprinkle over caramel layer, pressing down gently.

4. Bake 20 to 22 minutes or until golden brown. Cool completely in pan on wire rack. Cut into bars. *Makes 16 bars*

Turtle Brownies

1 package (18 ounces) refrigerated sugar cookie dough
⅓ cup unsweetened cocoa powder
1 egg, lightly beaten
10 caramels
2 tablespoons whipping cream
1 cup pecan halves, coarsely chopped

1. Preheat oven to 350°F. Lightly grease 11×7-inch baking pan. Let dough stand at room temperature about 15 minutes.

2. Beat dough, cocoa and egg in large bowl with electric mixer at medium speed until well blended. (Dough will be sticky.) Press dough into bottom of prepared pan. Bake 12 minutes.

3. Meanwhile, place caramels and cream in small microwavable bowl. Microwave on HIGH 3 minutes or until caramels are soft; stir until smooth.

4. Drop spoonfuls of caramel mixture over top of brownies; sprinkle with pecans. Bake 8 to 9 minutes or until center is set. Cool completely in pan on wire rack. Cut into bars.

Makes about 1 dozen brownies

Pecan Pie Bars

1 package (18 ounces) refrigerated sugar cookie dough
½ cup all-purpose flour
3 eggs
¾ cup sugar
¾ cup dark corn syrup
1 teaspoon vanilla
¼ teaspoon salt
3 cups chopped pecans

1. Preheat oven to 350°F. Lightly grease 13×9-inch baking pan. Let dough stand at room temperature about 15 minutes.

2. Beat dough and flour in large bowl with electric mixer at medium speed until well blended. Press dough into bottom of prepared pan. Bake 20 minutes.

3. Meanwhile, beat eggs in large bowl until fluffy and light in color. Add sugar, corn syrup, vanilla and salt; beat until well blended. Pour over crust; sprinkle evenly with pecans.

4. Bake 25 to 30 minutes or until center is just set. Cool completely in pan on wire rack. Cut into bars.   *Makes about 2 dozen bars*

Covetable
CAKES

Tropical Sunshine Cake

1 package (18.25 ounces) yellow cake mix
1 can (12 fluid ounces) NESTLÉ® CARNATION® Evaporated Milk
2 large eggs
1 can (20 ounces) crushed pineapple in juice, drained (juice reserved), divided
½ cup chopped almonds
¾ cup sifted powdered sugar
1 cup flaked coconut, toasted
    Whipped cream

PREHEAT oven to 350°F. Grease 13×9-inch baking pan.

COMBINE cake mix, evaporated milk and eggs in large mixer bowl. Beat on low speed for 2 minutes. Stir in *1 cup* pineapple. Pour batter into prepared baking pan. Sprinkle with almonds.

BAKE for 30 to 35 minutes or until wooden pick inserted in center comes out clean. Cool in pan on wire rack for 15 minutes.

COMBINE sugar and 2 tablespoons *reserved* pineapple juice in small bowl; mix until smooth. Spread over warm cake; sprinkle with coconut and *remaining* pineapple. Cool completely before serving. Top with whipped cream.   *Makes 12 servings*

Sweetheart Chocolate Mini Bundt Cakes

1⅔ cups all-purpose flour
½ cup unsweetened cocoa powder
1 teaspoon baking soda
¼ teaspoon salt
1 cup plus 2 tablespoons buttermilk
¾ cup packed brown sugar
¾ cup mayonnaise
1 teaspoon vanilla
1 cup semisweet chocolate chips, divided
¼ cup whipping cream

1. Preheat oven to 350°F. Spray 6 mini bundt pans with nonstick cooking spray.

2. Combine flour, cocoa, baking soda and salt in medium bowl. Beat buttermilk, brown sugar, mayonnaise and vanilla in large bowl with electric mixer at medium speed until well blended. Gradually add flour mixture; beat 2 minutes or until well blended. Stir in ½ cup chocolate chips.

3. Spoon batter evenly into prepared pans. Bake 22 minutes or until toothpick inserted near centers comes out clean. Cool in pans 15 minutes; invert onto wire rack to cool completely.

4. Place remaining ½ cup chocolate chips in small bowl. Heat cream in small saucepan over low heat until bubbles form around edge of pan; pour over chips. Let stand 5 minutes; stir until smooth. Cool until slightly thickened; drizzle over cakes.

Makes 6 mini bundt cakes

Delicious Strawberry Torte

4 eggs, separated
1 package (about 18 ounces) yellow cake mix
1⅓ cups milk
1 package (4-serving size) vanilla instant pudding and pie filling mix
¼ cup vegetable oil
1 teaspoon vanilla
1 container (16 ounces) vanilla frosting
1 quart strawberries, stemmed and halved
Whole strawberries (optional)

1. Preheat oven to 375°F. Grease and flour two 9-inch round cake pans.

2. Beat egg whites in medium bowl with electric mixer at high speed until soft peaks form. Beat cake mix, milk, pudding mix, egg yolks, oil and vanilla in large bowl at medium speed 2 minutes or until until well blended. Fold in egg whites. Pour batter into prepared pans.

3. Bake 28 to 32 minutes or until toothpick inserted into centers comes out clean. Cool in pans 15 minutes. Remove to wire racks; cool completely.

4. Cut each cake layer in half horizontally. Place 1 layer half on serving plate. Spread with one fourth of frosting; top with one third of strawberry halves. Repeat with remaining cake layer halves, frosting and strawberry halves, ending with frosting. Garnish top with whole strawberries. *Makes 10 to 12 servings*

German Upside Down Cake

1½ cups shredded coconut
 1 cup chopped pecans
 1 container (16 ounces) coconut pecan frosting
 1 package (about 18 ounces) German chocolate cake mix
1⅓ cups water
 4 eggs
 1 cup milk chocolate chips
 ⅓ cup vegetable oil
   Whipped cream (optional)

1. Preheat oven to 350°F. Spray 13×9-inch glass baking dish with nonstick cooking spray.

2. Spread coconut evenly in prepared pan. Sprinkle pecans over coconut. Spoon frosting by tablespoonfuls over pecans. (Do not spread.)

3. Beat cake mix, water, eggs, chocolate chips and oil in large bowl with electric mixer at low speed 30 seconds. Beat at medium speed 2 minutes or until well blended and creamy. Pour batter into prepared pan, spreading carefully over frosting.

4. Bake 35 to 40 minutes or until toothpick inserted into center comes out clean. Cool in pan 10 minutes; invert onto serving plate. Serve warm. Top with whipped cream, if desired. *Makes 12 to 15 servings*

Pink Lady Cake

**1 package (about 18 ounces) devil's food cake mix, plus ingredients
    to prepare mix
1 container (16 ounces) vanilla frosting
    Red food coloring
1 package (3 ounces) ladyfingers, split in half
    Pink satin ribbon (optional)**

1. Preheat oven to 350°F. Grease two 8-inch round cake pans.

2. Prepare cake mix according to package directions. Pour batter into prepared pans. Bake 30 minutes or until toothpick inserted into centers comes out clean. Cool completely in pans on wire racks.

3. Combine frosting and enough food coloring in large bowl until desired shade of pink is reached. Remove cake layers from pans. Place one layer on serving plate; spread with frosting. Top with second cake layer; frost top and side of cake.

4. Arrange ladyfingers around side of cake, pressing flat sides into frosting as shown in photo. Tie ribbon around cake, if desired.   *Makes 10 to 12 servings*

Red Velvet Cake

**2 packages (about 18 ounces each) white cake mix
2 teaspoons baking soda
3 cups buttermilk
4 eggs
2 bottles (1 ounce each) red food coloring
2 containers (16 ounces each) vanilla frosting**

1. Preheat oven to 350°F. Grease and flour four 9-inch round cake pans.

2. Combine cake mixes and baking soda in large bowl. Add buttermilk, eggs and food coloring; beat with electric mixer at low speed until moistened. Beat at high speed 2 minutes.

3. Pour batter into prepared pans. Bake 30 to 35 minutes or until toothpick inserted into centers comes out clean. Cool in pans 10 minutes. Remove to wire racks; cool completely.

4. Place one cake layer on serving plate; spread with frosting. Repeat with second and third cake layers. Top with fourth cake layer; frost top and side of cake.

Makes 16 servings

Tres Leches Cake

1 package (about 18 ounces) white cake mix, plus ingredients to prepare mix
1 can (14 ounces) sweetened condensed milk
1 cup milk
1 cup whipping cream
1 container (8 ounces) whipped topping, thawed
  Fresh fruit (optional)

1. Preheat oven to 350°F. Spray 13×9-inch baking pan with nonstick cooking spray.

2. Prepare cake mix according to package directions. Pour batter into prepared pan. Bake 35 to 40 minutes or until toothpick inserted into center comes out clean. Cool in pan 5 minutes.

3. Combine condensed milk, milk and whipping cream in 4-cup measure. Poke holes all over warm cake with wooden skewer or toothpick. Slowly pour milk mixture evenly over top of cake. Let cake stand 10 to 15 minutes to absorb liquid. Cover and refrigerate at least 1 hour.

4. When completely cool, spread whipped topping over cake. Garnish with fruit. Keep cake covered and refrigerated.   *Makes 12 to 15 servings*

Chocolate-Covered Coconut Almond Cake

¾ cup toasted sliced almonds, divided
1 package (about 18 ounces) yellow cake mix
1 package (4-serving size) vanilla instant pudding and pie filling mix
4 eggs
1 cup sour cream
¾ cup water
¼ cup vegetable oil
½ teaspoon vanilla
½ teaspoon coconut extract
⅔ cup shredded coconut, divided
½ cup whipping cream
½ cup semisweet chocolate chips

1. Preheat oven to 350°F. Spray 10- or 12-cup bundt pan with nonstick cooking spray. Coarsely chop ½ cup almonds.

2. Beat cake mix, pudding mix, eggs, sour cream, water, oil, vanilla and coconut extract in large bowl with electric mixer at low speed 30 seconds. Beat at medium speed 2 minutes. Fold in chopped almonds and ⅓ cup coconut. Pour batter into prepared pan. Bake 1 hour or until toothpick inserted near center comes out clean. Cool in pan 15 minutes; invert onto wire rack to cool completely.

3. Heat cream in small saucepan just until hot. (Do not boil.) Remove from heat; add chocolate chips and let stand 2 minutes. Whisk until smooth. Let stand at room temperature 15 minutes or until thickened. Stir; pour over cake. Sprinkle with remaining ¼ cup almonds and ⅓ cup coconut. Refrigerate until ready to serve.

Makes 10 to 12 servings

Apple Spice Custard Cake

1 (18.25-ounce) package spice cake mix
2 medium apples, peeled, cored and chopped
1 (14-ounce) can EAGLE BRAND® Sweetened Condensed Milk
    (NOT evaporated milk)
1 (8-ounce) container sour cream
¼ cup lemon juice
    Ground cinnamon (optional)

1. Preheat oven to 350°F. Grease and flour 13×9-inch baking pan.

2. Prepare cake mix according to package directions. Stir in apples. Pour batter into prepared pan. Bake 30 to 35 minutes or until toothpick inserted near center comes out clean.

3. In medium bowl, combine EAGLE BRAND® and sour cream; mix well. Stir in lemon juice. Remove cake from oven; spread sour cream mixture evenly over hot cake.

4. Return to oven; bake 5 minutes or until set. Sprinkle with cinnamon (optional). Cool. Chill. Store leftovers covered in refrigerator. *Makes one (13×9-inch) cake*

Prep Time: 15 minutes
Bake Time: 35 to 40 minutes

Easy Lemon Cake Roll

½ cup powdered sugar

1 package (about 16 ounces) angel food cake mix

1¼ cups water

1 package (4-serving size) lemon instant pudding and pie filling mix

2 cups cold milk

1 container (12 ounces) whipped topping, thawed

2 to 3 drops yellow food coloring (optional)

1½ cups shredded coconut

1. Preheat oven to 350°F. Spray 17×12-inch jelly-roll pan with nonstick cooking spray. Line with waxed paper. Sprinkle clean towel with powdered sugar.

2. Beat cake mix and water in large bowl according to package directions. Pour batter into prepared pan. Bake 17 minutes or until toothpick inserted into center comes out clean. Immediately invert cake onto prepared towel. Fold towel edge over cake and roll up cake and towel jelly-roll style. Place seam side down on wire rack to cool completely.

3. Combine pudding mix and milk in medium bowl; whisk 2 minutes or until thickened. Fold in whipped topping and food coloring, if desired. Refrigerate until ready to use.

4. Unroll cake, removing towel. Reserve 1 cup pudding; spread remaining pudding evenly onto cake. Re-roll cake; place seam side down on platter. (If cake breaks, hold pieces together and continue to roll.) Frost cake with reserved 1 cup pudding; sprinkle with coconut. Cut 1 inch off each end with serrated knife; discard scraps. Cover; refrigerate 2 to 3 hours before serving. *Makes 10 servings*

Peanut Butter & Cookie Cake

1 package (about 18 ounces) white cake mix
1 package (4-serving size) vanilla instant pudding and pie filling mix
4 eggs
½ cup milk
⅓ cup vegetable oil
¼ cup water
¼ cup creamy peanut butter
2 cups chopped peanut butter cookies, divided
½ cup semisweet chocolate chips
1 teaspoon shortening

1. Preheat oven to 350°F. Spray 12-cup bundt pan with nonstick cooking spray.

2. Beat cake mix, pudding mix, eggs, milk, oil, water and peanut butter in large bowl with electric mixer at medium speed 2 minutes or until well blended. Stir in 1¾ cups chopped cookies. Pour batter into prepared pan.

3. Bake 50 to 60 minutes or until toothpick inserted near center comes out clean. Cool in pan 15 minutes; invert onto wire rack to cool completely.

4. Combine chocolate chips and shortening in small microwavable bowl. Microwave on HIGH 1 minute; stir. Microwave at additional 15-second intervals until melted and smooth. Spoon glaze over cake; sprinkle with remaining ¼ cup chopped cookies.

Makes 10 to 12 servings

Chocolate Syrup Swirl Cake

1 cup (2 sticks) butter or margarine, softened
2 cups sugar
2 teaspoons vanilla extract
3 eggs
2¾ cups all-purpose flour
1¼ teaspoons baking soda, divided
½ teaspoon salt
1 cup buttermilk or sour milk*
1 cup HERSHEY'S Syrup
1 cup MOUNDS® Sweetened Coconut Flakes (optional)

To sour milk: Use 1 tablespoon white vinegar plus milk to equal 1 cup.

1. Heat oven to 350°F. Grease and flour a 12-cup fluted tube pan or 10-inch tube pan.

2. Beat butter, sugar and vanilla in large bowl until fluffy. Add eggs; beat well. Stir together flour, 1 teaspoon baking soda and salt; add alternately with buttermilk to butter mixture, beating until well blended.

3. Measure 2 cups batter in small bowl; stir in syrup and remaining ¼ teaspoon baking soda. Add coconut, if desired, to remaining vanilla batter; pour into prepared pan. Pour chocolate batter over vanilla batter in pan; do not mix.

4. Bake 60 to 70 minutes or until wooden pick inserted in center comes out clean. Cool 15 minutes; remove from pan to wire rack. Cool completely; glaze or frost as desired.   *Makes 20 servings*

Cookie
OVERLOAD

Carrot Cake Cookies

1½ cups all-purpose flour
1 teaspoon ground cinnamon
½ teaspoon baking soda
½ teaspoon salt
¾ cup packed brown sugar
½ cup (1 stick) butter, softened
1 egg
½ teaspoon vanilla
1 cup grated carrots (about 2 medium)
½ cup chopped walnuts
½ cup raisins or chopped dried pineapple (optional)

1. Preheat oven to 350°F. Grease cookie sheets or line with parchment paper.

2. Combine flour, cinnamon, baking soda and salt in medium bowl. Beat brown sugar and butter in large bowl with electric mixer at medium speed until creamy. Add egg and vanilla; beat until well blended. Beat in flour mixture. Stir in carrots, walnuts and raisins, if desired. Drop dough by rounded tablespoonfuls 2 inches apart onto prepared cookie sheets.

3. Bake 12 to 14 minutes or until set and edges are lightly browned. Cool on cookie sheets 1 minute. Remove to wire racks; cool completely.

Makes about 3 dozen cookies

Extra Chunky Peanut Butter Cookies

2 cups all-purpose flour
1 teaspoon baking soda
½ teaspoon salt
1 cup chunky peanut butter
¾ cup granulated sugar
½ cup packed light brown sugar
½ cup (1 stick) butter, softened
2 eggs
1 teaspoon vanilla
1½ cups chopped chocolate-covered peanut butter cups (12 to 14 candies)
1 cup dry roasted peanuts

1. Preheat oven to 350°F. Line cookie sheets with parchment paper or lightly grease.

2. Combine flour, baking soda and salt in medium bowl. Beat peanut butter, granulated sugar, brown sugar and butter in large bowl with electric mixer at medium speed until creamy. Beat in eggs and vanilla. Add flour mixture; beat until well blended. Stir in chopped candy and peanuts. Drop dough by rounded tablespoonfuls 2 inches apart on prepared cookie sheets.

3. Bake 13 minutes or until set. Cool on cookie sheets 1 minute. Remove to wire racks; cool completely.
Makes about 4 dozen cookies

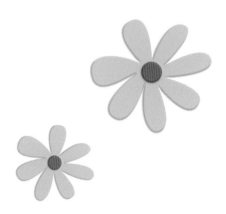

Chocolate Strawberry Stackers

2½ cups powdered sugar, divided
1 cup (2 sticks) plus 6 tablespoons unsalted butter, softened, divided
2 tablespoons packed light brown sugar
½ teaspoon salt, divided
2 cups all-purpose flour
½ cup semisweet chocolate chips, melted
⅓ cup strawberry jam
½ teaspoon vanilla
1 to 2 tablespoons milk (optional)

1. Beat ½ cup powdered sugar, 1 cup butter, brown sugar and ¼ teaspoon salt in large bowl with electric mixer at medium speed 2 minutes or until light and fluffy. Gradually add flour, beating well after each addition. Beat in melted chocolate until well blended. Shape dough into 14-inch log. Wrap in plastic wrap; refrigerate 1 hour.

2. Preheat oven to 300°F. Cut log into ⅓-inch-thick slices; place on ungreased cookie sheets. Bake 15 to 18 minutes or until set. Cool on cookie sheets 5 minutes. Remove to wire racks; cool completely.

3. Beat remaining 6 tablespoons butter in large bowl with electric mixer at medium speed until smooth. Beat in jam, vanilla and remaining ¼ teaspoon salt until blended. Gradually add remaining 2 cups powdered sugar; beat until fluffy. If mixture is too thick, gradually beat in milk until desired spreading consistency is reached. Spread frosting over flat sides of half of cookies; top with remaining cookies.

Makes about 20 sandwich cookies

Citrus Coolers

1½ cups powdered sugar
1 package (about 18 ounces) lemon cake mix
1 cup (4 ounces) pecan pieces
½ cup all-purpose flour
½ cup (1 stick) butter, melted
  Grated peel and juice of 1 large orange

1. Preheat oven to 375°F. Line cookie sheets with parchment paper. Place powdered sugar in medium bowl; set aside.

2. Beat cake mix, pecans, flour, butter, orange peel and juice in large bowl with electric mixer at medium speed until well blended. Drop dough by rounded tablespoonfuls 2 inches apart onto prepared cookie sheets.

3. Bake 13 to 15 minutes or until bottoms are light golden brown. Cool on cookie sheets 3 minutes; roll in powdered sugar. Remove to wire racks; cool completely.

Makes about 4½ dozen cookies

Prep Time: 10 minutes
Bake Time: 13 to 15 minutes

Caramel-Kissed Pecan Cookies

1 package (18 ounces) refrigerated sugar cookie dough
½ cup all-purpose flour
1 package (2 ounces) ground pecans
12 caramel-filled milk chocolate kiss candies, unwrapped
1 package (2 ounces) pecan chips
  Caramel ice cream topping (optional)

1. Preheat oven to 350°F. Line cookie sheet with parchment paper. Let dough stand at room temperature 15 minutes.

2. Beat cookie dough, flour and ground pecans in medium bowl with electric mixer at medium speed until well blended. Divide into 12 equal pieces. Place one candy in center of each piece of dough. Shape dough into ball around candies; seal well. Roll each ball in pecan chips. Place 2 inches apart on cookie sheet.

3. Bake 16 to 18 minutes or until light golden around edges. Cool on cookie sheet 2 minutes.

4. If desired, warm caramel topping according to package directions. Drizzle over warm cookies. Remove to wire rack; cool completely. Store in airtight container.

Makes 1 dozen cookies

Waikiki Cookies

1½ cups packed light brown sugar
⅔ cup shortening
1 tablespoon water
1 teaspoon vanilla
2 eggs
1¾ cups all-purpose flour
½ teaspoon salt
¼ teaspoon baking soda
1 cup white chocolate chunks
1 cup macadamia nuts, coarsely chopped

1. Preheat oven to 375°F.

2. Beat brown sugar, shortening, water and vanilla in large bowl with electric mixer at medium speed until well blended. Add eggs; beat well.

3. Combine flour, salt and baking soda in medium bowl. Add to sugar mixture; beat at low speed just until blended. Stir in white chocolate chunks and nuts.

4. Drop dough by rounded tablespoonfuls 2 inches apart onto ungreased cookie sheets.

5. Bake 7 to 9 minutes or until set. (Do not overbake.) Cool on cookie sheets 2 minutes. Remove to wire racks; cool completely.   *Makes about 3 dozen cookies*

Chocolate Chunk Cookies

1⅔ cups all-purpose flour
⅓ cup CREAM OF WHEAT® Hot Cereal (Instant, 1-minute, 2½-minute or 10-minute cook time), uncooked
½ teaspoon baking soda
¼ teaspoon salt
¾ cup (1½ sticks) butter, softened
½ cup packed brown sugar
⅓ cup granulated sugar
1 egg
1 teaspoon vanilla extract
1 (11.5-ounce) bag chocolate chunks
1 cup chopped pecans

1. Preheat oven to 375°F. Lightly grease cookie sheets. Blend flour, Cream of Wheat, baking soda and salt in medium bowl; set aside.

2. Beat butter and sugars in large bowl with electric mixer at medium speed until creamy. Add egg and vanilla. Beat until fluffy. Reduce speed to low. Add Cream of Wheat mixture; mix well. Stir in chocolate chunks and pecans.

3. Drop by tablespoonfuls onto prepared cookie sheets. Bake 9 to 11 minutes or until golden brown. Let stand on cookie sheets 1 minute before transferring to wire racks to cool completely.   *Makes 24 cookies*

Tip: For a colorful item to take to school bake sales or give as a gift, replace the chocolate chunks with multicolored candy-coated chocolate.

Gingery Oat and Molasses Cookies

1 cup all-purpose flour
¾ cup whole wheat flour
½ cup uncooked old-fashioned oats
1½ teaspoons baking powder
1½ teaspoons ground ginger
1 teaspoon baking soda
½ teaspoon ground cinnamon
¼ teaspoon salt
¾ cup sugar
½ cup (1 stick) unsalted butter, softened
1 egg
¼ cup molasses
¼ teaspoon vanilla
1 cup chopped crystallized ginger
½ cup chopped walnuts

1. Combine all-purpose flour, whole wheat flour, oats, baking powder, ground ginger, baking soda, cinnamon and salt in large bowl.

2. Beat sugar and butter in large bowl with electric mixer at high speed until light and fluffy. Beat in egg, molasses and vanilla. Gradually beat in flour mixture. Stir in crystallized ginger and walnuts. Shape into 2 logs about 8 to 10 inches long. Wrap in plastic wrap and chill 1 to 3 hours.

3. Preheat oven to 350°F. Grease cookie sheets. Cut logs into ⅓-inch slices. Place 1½ inches apart on prepared cookie sheets. Bake 12 to 14 minutes or until set and browned at edges. Cool on cookie sheets 5 minutes. Remove to wire racks; cool completely. *Makes about 4 dozen cookies*

Pumpkin Chocolate Chip Sandwiches

1 cup solid-pack pumpkin
1 package (18 ounces) refrigerated chocolate chip cookie dough
¾ cup all-purpose flour
½ teaspoon pumpkin pie spice*
½ cup prepared cream cheese frosting

You may substitute ¼ teaspoon ground cinnamon, ⅛ teaspoon ground ginger and pinch each ground allspice and ground nutmeg for ½ teaspoon pumpkin pie spice.

1. Line colander with paper towel. Place pumpkin in colander; drain about 20 minutes to remove excess moisture.

2. Preheat oven to 350°F. Grease cookie sheets. Let dough stand at room temperature 15 minutes.

3. Beat dough, pumpkin, flour and pumpkin pie spice in large bowl with electric mixer at medium speed until well blended.

4. Drop dough by rounded teaspoonfuls 2 inches apart onto prepared cookie sheets. Bake 9 to 11 minutes or until set. Cool on cookie sheets 3 minutes. Remove to wire racks; cool completely.

5. Spread about 1 teaspoon frosting on flat side of one cookie; top with second cookie. Repeat with remaining frosting and cookies.   *Makes about 2 dozen sandwich cookies*

Holiday Treasure Cookies

1½ cups graham cracker crumbs
½ cup all-purpose flour
2 teaspoons baking powder
1 (14-ounce) can EAGLE BRAND® Sweetened Condensed Milk
    (NOT evaporated milk)
½ cup (1 stick) butter or margarine, softened
1⅓ cups flaked coconut
1¾ cups (10 ounces) mini kisses, milk chocolate or semisweet chocolate
    baking pieces
1 cup red and green holiday baking bits

1. Preheat oven to 375°F. In medium bowl, combine graham cracker crumbs, flour and baking powder; set aside.

2. Beat EAGLE BRAND® and butter until smooth; add reserved crumb mixture, mixing well. Stir in coconut, chocolate pieces and holiday baking bits. Drop by rounded teaspoonfuls onto greased cookie sheets.

3. Bake 7 to 9 minutes or until lightly browned. Cool 1 minute; transfer from cookie sheet to wire rack. Cool completely. Store leftovers tightly covered at room temperature.   *Makes about 5½ dozen cookies*

Prep Time: 10 minutes
Bake Time: 7 to 9 minutes

Cinnamon Raisin Delights

1¼ cups all-purpose flour
1 teaspoon ground cinnamon
½ teaspoon salt
½ teaspoon baking soda
½ cup (1 stick) butter, softened
½ cup packed light brown sugar
¼ cup granulated sugar
1 egg, lightly beaten
1 teaspoon vanilla
1 cup raisins
¾ cup prepared vanilla frosting

1. Preheat oven to 350°F. Lightly grease cookie sheets.

2. Combine flour, cinnamon, salt and baking soda in medium bowl. Beat butter, brown sugar and granulated sugar in large bowl with electric mixer at medium speed until light and fluffy. Add egg and vanilla; beat until well blended. Add flour mixture; beat just until blended. Stir in raisins.

3. Shape dough by rounded tablespoonfuls into balls; place 2 inches apart on prepared cookie sheets.

4. Bake 11 to 13 minutes or until edges are lightly browned. Cool on cookie sheets 2 minutes. Remove to wire racks; cool completely.

5. Spread 1 tablespoon frosting on flat side of one cookie; top with second cookie. Repeat with remaining cookies and frosting.   *Makes about 1 dozen sandwich cookies*

Malted Milk Cookies

1 cup (2 sticks) butter, softened
¾ cup granulated sugar
¾ cup packed light brown sugar
1 teaspoon baking soda
2 eggs
2 squares (1 ounce each) unsweetened chocolate, melted and
    cooled to room temperature
1 teaspoon vanilla
2¼ cups all-purpose flour
½ cup malted milk powder
1 cup chopped malted milk balls

1. Preheat oven to 375°F.

2. Beat butter in large bowl with electric mixer at medium speed until creamy.
Add granulated sugar, brown sugar and baking soda; beat until blended. Add eggs,
chocolate and vanilla; beat until well blended. Beat in flour and malted milk powder
until blended. Stir in malted milk balls. Drop dough by rounded tablespoonfuls
2½ inches apart onto ungreased cookie sheets.

3. Bake 10 minutes or until edges are set. Cool on cookie sheets 1 minute. Remove to
wire racks; cool completely.   *Makes about 3 dozen cookies*

The publisher would like to thank the companies and organizations listed below for the use of their recipes in this publication.

ACH Food Companies, Inc.

Cabot® Creamery Cooperative

Cream of Wheat® Cereal

Dole Food Company, Inc.

EAGLE BRAND®

The Hershey Company

Nestlé USA

Recipes to Share Notes

Spiced Orange Cranberry Muffins

Blueberry Cinnamon Muffins

½ cup dried cranberries
3 tablespoons packed brown sugar
1 cup orange juice
1 egg white
2 tablespoons canola or vegetable oil

1 cup whole wheat flour
½ cup all-purpose flour
1½ teaspoons baking powder
½ teaspoon ground cinnamon
¼ teaspoon ground nutmeg

1. Preheat oven to 400°F. Grease 8 standard (2½-inch) muffin cups or line with paper baking cups. Combine cranberries and brown sugar in small bowl. Stir in orange juice, egg white and oil; let stand 5 minutes.

2. Combine whole wheat flour, all-purpose flour, baking powder, cinnamon and nutmeg in medium bowl. Add cranberry mixture to flour mixture; stir just until combined. Spoon batter into prepared muffin cups, filling three-fourths full.

3. Bake 18 to 20 minutes or until toothpick inserted into centers comes out clean. Immediately remove from pan; cool completely on wire rack.   *Makes 8 muffins*

1¼ cups all-purpose flour
½ cup CREAM OF WHEAT®
   Cinnamon Swirl Instant Hot
   Cereal, uncooked
½ cup sugar, divided
1 tablespoon baking powder
2 teaspoons ground cinnamon

½ teaspoon salt
1 cup fat-free milk
1 egg
2 tablespoons oil
1 teaspoon vanilla extract
1 cup fresh or frozen blueberries
2 tablespoons apple juice

1. Preheat oven to 400°F. Grease 12 (2½-inch) muffin cups. Mix flour, Cream of Wheat, ¼ cup sugar, baking powder, cinnamon and salt in medium bowl; set aside.

2. Beat milk, egg, oil and vanilla with wire whisk in separate bowl until well blended. Add to dry ingredients; stir just until moistened. Gently stir in blueberries. Spoon evenly into prepared muffin cups, filling each cup two-thirds full.

3. Bake 18 to 20 minutes or until toothpick inserted into centers comes out clean. Remove muffins from pan.

4. Brush tops of warm muffins with apple juice; roll in remaining ¼ cup sugar. Serve warm.   *Makes 12 muffins*

Tip: To make Strawberries 'n Cream Muffins, use CREAM OF WHEAT® Strawberries 'n Cream Instant Hot Cereal and frozen strawberries.

Piña Colada Muffins

Ginger Squash Muffins

2 cups all-purpose flour
¾ cup sugar
½ cup flaked coconut
2 teaspoons baking powder
½ teaspoon baking soda
½ teaspoon salt
2 eggs

1 cup sour cream
1 can (8 ounces) crushed pineapple
    in juice, undrained
¼ cup (½ stick) butter, melted
⅛ teaspoon coconut extract
Additional flaked coconut
    (optional)

1. Preheat oven to 400°F. Spray 18 standard (2½-inch) muffin cups with nonstick cooking spray or line with paper baking cups.

2. Combine flour, sugar, coconut, baking powder, baking soda and salt in large bowl; mix well.

3. Beat eggs in medium bowl with electric mixer at medium speed 1 to 2 minutes or until frothy. Beat in sour cream, pineapple with juice, butter and coconut extract. Add to flour mixture; beat just until combined. Spoon batter into prepared muffin cups, filling three-fourths full.

4. Bake 15 to 20 minutes or until toothpick inserted into centers comes out clean. If desired, sprinkle tops of muffins with additional coconut after first 10 minutes. Cool in pans 2 minutes. Remove to wire racks; cool completely.   *Makes 18 muffins*

1½ cups all-purpose flour
⅓ cup whole wheat flour
⅓ cup granulated sugar
¼ cup packed dark brown sugar
2½ teaspoons baking powder
1 teaspoon ground cinnamon
½ teaspoon baking soda
½ teaspoon salt

½ teaspoon ground ginger
1 cup frozen winter squash,* thawed
2 eggs, beaten
⅓ cup canola oil
¼ cup finely chopped walnuts
2 tablespoons finely chopped
    crystallized ginger (optional)

One 12-ounce package frozen squash yields about 1 cup squash.

1. Preheat oven to 375°F. Spray 12 standard (2½-inch) muffin cups with nonstick cooking spray.

2. Combine all-purpose flour, whole wheat flour, granulated sugar, brown sugar, baking powder, cinnamon, baking soda, salt and ground ginger in large bowl; mix well.

3. Combine squash, eggs and oil in small bowl. Add to flour mixture; stir just until blended. (Do not beat.) Stir in walnuts and crystallized ginger, if desired. Spoon batter into prepared muffin cups, filling two-thirds full.

4. Bake 18 to 20 minutes or until toothpick inserted into centers comes out clean. Cool in pan 5 minutes. Remove to wire rack; cool completely.   *Makes 12 muffins*

Banana Peanut Butter Chip Muffins

Toffee Crunch Muffins

2 cups all-purpose flour
¾ cup sugar
2 teaspoons baking powder
½ teaspoon baking soda
¼ teaspoon salt
1 cup mashed ripe bananas (about 2 large)

½ cup (1 stick) butter, melted
2 eggs, beaten
⅓ cup buttermilk
1½ teaspoons vanilla
1 cup peanut butter chips
½ cup chopped peanuts

1. Preheat oven to 375°F. Grease 15 standard (2½-inch) muffins cups or line with paper baking cups.

2. Combine flour, sugar, baking powder, baking soda and salt in large bowl. Whisk bananas, butter, eggs, buttermilk and vanilla in medium bowl until well blended.

3. Add banana mixture to flour mixture; stir just until blended. Gently fold in peanut butter chips. Spoon batter into prepared muffin cups, filling three-fourths full. Sprinkle with chopped peanuts.

4. Bake 20 minutes or until toothpick inserted into centers comes out clean. Cool in pans 2 minutes. Remove to wire racks; cool completely. *Makes 15 muffins*

Tip: Substitute a mixture of chocolate chips and peanut butter chips for the peanut butter chips for a combination of three great flavors in one muffin.

1½ cups all-purpose flour
⅓ cup packed brown sugar
2 teaspoons baking powder
½ teaspoon baking soda
½ teaspoon salt
½ cup milk

½ cup sour cream
1 egg, beaten
3 tablespoons butter, melted
1 teaspoon vanilla
3 bars (1.4 ounces each) chocolate-covered toffee, chopped, divided

1. Preheat oven to 400°F. Grease 36 mini (1¾-inch) muffin cups or line with paper baking cups.

2. Combine flour, brown sugar, baking powder, baking soda and salt in large bowl. Combine milk, sour cream, egg, butter and vanilla in small bowl until well blended. Stir into flour mixture just until moistened. Fold in two thirds of toffee. Spoon batter into prepared muffin cups, filling almost full. Sprinkle evenly with remaining toffee.

3. Bake 16 to 18 minutes or until toothpick inserted into centers comes out clean. Cool in pans 2 minutes. Remove to wire racks; cool completely. *Makes 36 mini muffins*

Variation: For larger muffins, spoon batter into 10 standard (2½-inch) greased or paper-lined muffin cups. Bake at 350°F 20 minutes or until toothpick inserted into centers comes out clean. Makes 10 muffins.

Apple-Cheddar Muffins

Photo © 2009 Publications International, Ltd.   Design © 2009 Publications International, Ltd.   Recipe © 2009 Cabot® Creamery Cooperative

Chocolate Chip Muffins

Photo © 2009 Publications International, Ltd.   Design © 2009 Publications International, Ltd.   Recipe © 2009 Publications International, Ltd.

1 cup whole wheat flour
1 cup all-purpose flour
2 tablespoons sugar
1 tablespoon baking powder
½ teaspoon salt
1 cup peeled, chopped apple
1 cup grated CABOT® Mild or Sharp Cheddar
2 eggs
1 cup milk
4 tablespoons CABOT® Salted Butter, melted

1. Preheat oven to 400°F. Butter 12 muffin cups or coat with nonstick cooking spray.

2. In mixing bowl, stir together whole wheat and white flour, sugar, baking powder and salt. Add apples and cheese and toss to combine.

3. In another bowl, whisk eggs lightly. Whisk in milk and butter. Make well in center of dry ingredients; add milk mixture and gently stir in dry ingredients from side until just combined.

4. Divide batter among prepared muffin cups. Bake for 20 minutes, or until muffins feel firm when lightly pressed on top. *Makes 12 muffins*

1¾ cups all-purpose flour
⅓ cup packed brown sugar
2 tablespoons unsweetened cocoa powder
2½ teaspoons baking powder
1½ teaspoons ground cinnamon
¼ teaspoon salt
1 cup milk
1 egg, lightly beaten
¼ cup unsweetened applesauce
2 tablespoons butter, melted
1 teaspoon vanilla
⅔ cup mini semisweet chocolate chips

1. Preheat oven to 400°F. Spray 12 standard (2½-inch) muffin cups with nonstick cooking spray or line with foil baking cups.

2. Combine flour, brown sugar, cocoa, baking powder, cinnamon and salt in medium bowl. Stir together milk, egg, applesauce, butter and vanilla in small bowl until blended. Add to flour mixture; stir just until blended. Fold in chocolate chips. Spoon batter evenly into prepared muffin cups.

3. Bake 13 to 15 minutes or until toothpick inserted into centers comes out clean. Cool in pan 5 minutes. Remove to wire rack; cool completely. *Makes 12 muffins*

Maple Magic Muffins

Orange-Raisin Bran Muffins

½ cup plus 3 tablespoons maple
  syrup,* divided
¼ cup chopped walnuts
2 tablespoons butter, melted
2 cups all-purpose flour
¾ cup sugar
2 teaspoons baking powder

½ teaspoon baking soda
½ teaspoon salt
¼ teaspoon ground cinnamon
¾ cup plus 1 tablespoon milk
½ cup vegetable oil
1 egg
½ teaspoon vanilla

For best flavor and texture, use pure maple syrup, not pancake syrup.

1. Preheat oven to 400°F. Grease 12 standard (2½-inch) nonstick muffin cups.
Place 2 teaspoons maple syrup, 1 teaspoon walnuts and ½ teaspoon melted butter
in each cup.

2. Combine flour, sugar, baking powder, baking soda, salt and cinnamon in large bowl;
mix well.

3. Whisk milk, oil, egg, remaining 3 tablespoons maple syrup and vanilla in medium
bowl until well blended. Add to flour mixture; stir just until blended. Spoon batter into
prepared muffin cups, filling two-thirds full. Place muffin pan on baking sheet to catch
any drips (maple syrup may overflow slightly).

4. Bake 20 to 25 minutes or until toothpick inserted into centers comes out clean. Invert
pan onto wire rack covered with waxed paper. Cool muffins slightly; serve warm.

Makes 12 muffins

MAZOLA PURE® Cooking Spray
⅓ cup boiling water
1 cup natural high-fiber bran cereal
  shreds
½ cup orange juice
1 egg
½ cup KARO® Light or Dark Corn
  Syrup

¼ cup sugar
¼ cup MAZOLA® Oil
½ cup raisins
1 cup flour
1 teaspoon baking soda
¼ teaspoon salt

1. Preheat oven to 400°F. Spray 12 (2½-inch) muffin pan cups with cooking spray. In
large bowl pour boiling water over cereal; let stand 2 minutes. Stir in orange juice, egg,
corn syrup, sugar, oil and raisins.

2. In medium bowl combine flour, baking soda and salt; set aside. Stir flour mixture into
cereal mixture until well blended. Spoon into prepared muffin pan cups.

3. Bake 15 to 20 minutes or until lightly browned and firm to touch. Cool in pan on
wire rack 5 minutes; remove from pan.

Makes 12 muffins

Sweet Potato Muffins

Pineapple Carrot Raisin Muffins

2 cups all-purpose flour
¾ cup chopped walnuts
¾ cup golden raisins
½ cup packed brown sugar
1 tablespoon baking powder
1 teaspoon ground cinnamon
½ teaspoon salt

½ teaspoon baking soda
¼ teaspoon ground nutmeg
1 cup mashed cooked sweet potato
¾ cup milk
½ cup (1 stick) butter, melted
2 eggs, beaten
1½ teaspoons vanilla

1. Preheat oven to 400°F. Grease 24 standard (2½-inch) muffin cups.

2. Combine flour, walnuts, raisins, brown sugar, baking powder, cinnamon, salt, baking soda and nutmeg in medium bowl; stir until well blended.

3. Combine sweet potato, milk, butter, eggs and vanilla in large bowl; stir until well blended. Add flour mixture to sweet potato mixture; stir just until dry ingredients are moistened. Spoon batter evenly into prepared muffin cups.

4. Bake 15 minutes or until toothpick inserted into centers comes out clean. Cool in pans 5 minutes. Remove to wire racks; cool completely.   *Makes 24 muffins*

---

2 cups all-purpose flour
1 cup sugar
1½ teaspoons baking powder
1 teaspoon ground cinnamon
1 can (8 ounces) DOLE® Crushed Pineapple, undrained

2 eggs
½ cup (1 stick) butter or margarine, melted
1 cup DOLE® Seedless or Golden Raisins
½ cup shredded DOLE® Carrots

• Combine flour, sugar, baking powder and cinnamon in large bowl.

• Add undrained pineapple, eggs, butter, raisins and carrots; stir just until blended.

• Spoon evenly into 36 mini-muffin cups sprayed with nonstick vegetable cooking spray.

• Bake at 375°F., 15 to 20 minutes or until toothpick inserted in center comes out clean. Remove muffins from pans onto wire rack to cool.   *Makes 3 dozen mini-muffins*

For 2½-inch Muffins: Spoon batter into 2½-inch muffin pans instead of mini-muffin pans. Bake as directed for 20 to 25 minutes. Cool as directed.

Gooey Caramel Chocolate Bars

Apricot Shortbread Diamonds

2 cups all-purpose flour
1 cup granulated sugar
¼ teaspoon salt
2 cups (4 sticks) butter, divided

1 cup packed light brown sugar
⅓ cup light corn syrup
1 cup (6 ounces) semisweet chocolate chips

1. Preheat oven to 350°F. Line 13×9-inch baking pan with foil. Combine flour, granulated sugar and salt in medium bowl. Cut in 14 tablespoons (1¾ sticks) butter until mixture resembles coarse crumbs. Press onto bottom of prepared pan.

2. Bake 18 to 20 minutes or until lightly browned around edges. Cool completely in pan on wire rack.

3. Combine 1 cup (2 sticks) butter, brown sugar and corn syrup in medium heavy saucepan. Cook over medium heat 5 to 8 minutes or until mixture boils, stirring frequently. Boil gently 2 minutes without stirring. Immediately pour over cooled base; spread evenly to edges of pan. Cool completely.

4. Melt chocolate and remaining 2 tablespoons butter in double boiler over simmering water. Pour over caramel layer; spread evenly to edges of pan. Refrigerate 10 minutes or until chocolate begins to set. Cool completely at room temperature. Remove foil; cut into bars.

Makes 3 dozen bars

---

1 package (about 18 ounces) yellow cake mix
2 eggs
¼ cup vegetable oil
1 tablespoon water

1 cup apricot jam or orange marmalade
1 cup diced dried apricots (about 6 ounces)
1 cup sliced almonds

1. Preheat oven to 350°F. Line 15×10-inch jelly-roll pan with foil and spray lightly with nonstick cooking spray.

2. Beat cake mix, eggs, oil and water in large bowl with electric mixer at medium speed until well blended. With damp hands, press dough into prepared pan.

3. Place jam in small microwavable bowl. Heat on HIGH 20 seconds to soften. Spread jam evenly over dough; sprinkle apricots and almonds over top.

4. Bake 25 minutes or until edges are browned and jam bubbles at edges. Cool completely in pan on wire rack. Remove foil; cut into diamond-shaped bars.

Makes about 2 dozen bars

Butterscotch Toffee Gingersnap Squares

O'Henrietta Bars

40 gingersnap cookies
⅓ cup butter, melted
1 can (14 ounces) sweetened
    condensed milk
1½ teaspoons vanilla
1 cup butterscotch chips

½ cup pecan pieces
½ cup chopped peanuts
½ cup milk chocolate toffee bits
½ cup mini semisweet chocolate
    chips

1. Preheat oven to 350°F. Line 13×9-inch baking pan with foil, leaving 1-inch overhang. Spray foil with nonstick cooking spray.

2. Place cookies in food processor; process until crumbs form. Combine 2 cups crumbs and butter in medium bowl; mix well. Press crumb mixture evenly into bottom of prepared pan. Bake 4 to 5 minutes or until light brown around edges.

3. Combine condensed milk and vanilla in small bowl; pour over warm crust. Sprinkle with butterscotch chips, pecans, peanuts, toffee bits and chocolate chips. Press down gently.

4. Bake 15 to 18 minutes or until bubbly and golden. Cool completely in pan on wire rack. Remove foil; cut into bars. Store in airtight container. *Makes 3 dozen bars*

MAZOLA PURE® Cooking Spray
½ cup (1 stick) butter or margarine,
    softened
½ cup packed brown sugar
½ cup KARO® Light or Dark Corn
    Syrup

1 teaspoon vanilla
3 cups quick oats, uncooked
½ cup (3 ounces) semi-sweet
    chocolate chips
¼ cup creamy peanut butter

1. Preheat oven to 350°F. Spray 8- or 9-inch square baking pan with cooking spray.

2. Beat butter, brown sugar, corn syrup and vanilla in large bowl with mixer at medium speed until smooth. Stir in oats. Press into prepared pan.

3. Bake 25 minutes or until center is barely firm. Cool on wire rack 5 minutes.

4. Sprinkle with chocolate chips; top with small spoonfuls of peanut butter. Let stand 5 minutes; spread peanut butter and chocolate over bars, swirling to marble.

5. Cool completely on wire rack before cutting. Cut into bars; refrigerate 15 minutes to set topping. *Makes 24 bars*

Cinnamon Apple Pie Bars

PB&J Cookie Bars

1 package (about 18 ounces) spice
  cake mix with pudding in
  the mix
2 cups uncooked old-fashioned oats
½ teaspoon ground cinnamon

¾ cup (1½ sticks) cold butter,
  cut into pieces
1 egg
1 can (21 ounces) apple pie filling
  and topping

1. Preheat oven to 350°F. Spray 13×9-inch baking pan with nonstick cooking spray.

2. Combine cake mix, oats and cinnamon in large bowl. Cut in butter using pastry blender or fingers until butter is evenly distributed and no large pieces remain (mixture will be dry and have clumps). Stir in egg until well mixed.

3. With damp hands, press about three-fourths oat mixture into bottom of prepared pan. Spread apple pie filling evenly over top. Crumble remaining oat mixture over filling. Bake 25 to 30 minutes or until top and edges are lightly browned. Cool completely in pan on wire rack. Cut into bars.   *Makes about 2 dozen bars*

1 package (about 18 ounces) yellow
  cake mix with pudding in
  the mix
1 cup peanut butter

½ cup vegetable oil
2 eggs
1 cup strawberry jam
1 cup peanut butter chips

1. Preheat oven to 350°F. Line 15×10-inch jelly-roll pan with foil and spray lightly with nonstick cooking spray.

2. Beat cake mix, peanut butter, oil and eggs in large bowl with electric mixer at medium speed until well blended. With damp hands, press mixture evenly into prepared pan. Bake 20 minutes.

3. Meanwhile, place jam in small microwavable bowl; heat on HIGH 20 seconds to soften. Spread jam evenly over cookie base. Scatter peanut butter chips over top.

4. Bake 10 minutes or until edges are browned. Cool completely in pan on wire rack. Remove foil; cut into bars.   *Makes about 3 dozen bars*

Black Forest Bars

Taffy Apple Bars

1 package (about 18 ounces) dark chocolate cake mix

½ cup (1 stick) unsalted butter, melted

1 egg

½ teaspoon almond extract

1¼ cup sliced almonds, divided

1 jar (about 16 ounces) maraschino cherries, well drained

½ cup semisweet chocolate chips

1. Preheat oven to 350°F. Line 13×9-inch baking pan with foil.

2. Beat cake mix, butter, egg and almond extract in large bowl with electric mixer at medium speed. Stir in ¾ cup almonds.

3. Press dough into bottom of prepared pan. Top evenly with cherries. Bake 20 to 25 minutes or until toothpick inserted into center comes out clean. Cool completely in pan on wire rack.

4. Place chocolate chips in small resealable food storage bag; seal bag. Microwave on HIGH 1 to 1½ minutes, kneading bag every 30 seconds until melted and smooth. Cut tiny corner from bag; drizzle chocolate over top. Sprinkle with remaining ½ cup almonds. Remove foil; cut into bars.   *Makes about 2 dozen bars*

---

1 package (18 ounces) refrigerated sugar cookie dough

1 package (18 ounces) refrigerated peanut butter cookie dough

½ cup all-purpose flour

3½ to 4 cups chopped cored peeled apples (about 2 large)

1 cup chopped peanuts

½ cup caramel ice cream topping

1. Preheat oven to 350°F. Lightly grease 13×9-inch baking pan. Let doughs stand at room temperature 15 minutes.

2. Beat doughs and flour in large bowl with electric mixer at medium speed until well blended. Press dough into bottom of prepared pan. Layer apples evenly over dough; press down lightly. Sprinkle with peanuts.

3. Bake 35 minutes or until edges are browned and center is firm to the touch. Cool completely in pan on wire rack. Drizzle with caramel topping. Cut into bars.   *Makes about 2 dozen bars*

Gingerbread Cheesecake Bars

Chocolate Oatmeal Caramel Bars

1 package (8 ounces) cream cheese, softened
⅔ cup sugar, divided
3 eggs
1½ teaspoons ground ginger, divided
½ teaspoon vanilla
½ cup (1 stick) butter, softened

¾ cup molasses
2 cups all-purpose flour
1 teaspoon baking soda
¾ teaspoon ground cinnamon
¼ teaspoon salt
¼ teaspoon ground allspice

1. Preheat oven to 350°F. Grease 13×9-inch baking pan.

2. Beat cream cheese and ⅓ cup sugar in medium bowl with electric mixer at medium speed until light and fluffy. Add 1 egg, ½ teaspoon ginger and vanilla; beat until well blended and smooth. Refrigerate until ready to use.

3. Beat butter and remaining ⅓ cup sugar in large bowl at medium speed until light and fluffy. Add molasses and remaining 2 eggs; beat until well blended. Combine flour, baking soda, remaining 1 teaspoon ginger, cinnamon, salt and allspice in medium bowl. Add flour mixture to butter mixture; beat just until blended. Spread batter evenly in prepared pan. Drop cream cheese mixture by spoonfuls onto gingerbread batter; swirl into batter with knife.

4. Bake 25 to 30 minutes or until toothpick inserted into center comes out clean. Cool completely in pan on wire rack. Cut into bars. *Makes 2 dozen bars*

1¼ cups uncooked old-fashioned oats
1 cup all-purpose flour
½ cup plus 2 tablespoons packed brown sugar, divided
2 tablespoons unsweetened Dutch process cocoa powder*

¾ cup (1½ sticks) butter, melted
1 can (14 ounces) sweetened condensed milk
⅓ cup butter
½ cup chopped pecans

While Dutch process cocoa powder has a stronger flavor and will bake a darker color, natural unsweetened cocoa powder may be substituted.

1. Preheat oven to 350°F. Combine oats, flour, ½ cup brown sugar and cocoa in medium bowl. Add ¾ cup melted butter; mix until crumbly. Reserve 1 cup oat mixture for topping; press remaining oat mixture into bottom of ungreased 8-inch square baking pan. Bake 15 minutes.

2. Meanwhile, combine condensed milk, ⅓ cup butter and remaining 2 tablespoons brown sugar in medium saucepan; cook and stir over medium heat 10 minutes or until thick and pale brown in color.

3. Cool milk mixture slightly until thickened; spread evenly over baked crust. Let stand 5 minutes or until set. Add pecans to reserved oat mixture; sprinkle over caramel layer, pressing down gently.

4. Bake 20 to 22 minutes or until golden brown. Cool completely in pan on wire rack. Cut into bars. *Makes 16 bars*

Turtle Brownies

Pecan Pie Bars

1 package (18 ounces) refrigerated
  sugar cookie dough
⅓ cup unsweetened cocoa powder
1 egg, lightly beaten

10 caramels
2 tablespoons whipping cream
1 cup pecan halves, coarsely chopped

1. Preheat oven to 350°F. Lightly grease 11×7-inch baking pan. Let dough stand at room temperature about 15 minutes.

2. Beat dough, cocoa and egg in large bowl with electric mixer at medium speed until well blended. (Dough will be sticky.) Press dough into bottom of prepared pan. Bake 12 minutes.

3. Meanwhile, place caramels and cream in small microwavable bowl. Microwave on HIGH 3 minutes or until caramels are soft; stir until smooth.

4. Drop spoonfuls of caramel mixture over top of brownies; sprinkle with pecans. Bake 8 to 9 minutes or until center is set. Cool completely in pan on wire rack. Cut into bars.   *Makes about 1 dozen brownies*

---

1 package (18 ounces) refrigerated
  sugar cookie dough
½ cup all-purpose flour
3 eggs
¾ cup sugar

¾ cup dark corn syrup
1 teaspoon vanilla
¼ teaspoon salt
3 cups chopped pecans

1. Preheat oven to 350°F. Lightly grease 13×9-inch baking pan. Let dough stand at room temperature about 15 minutes.

2. Beat dough and flour in large bowl with electric mixer at medium speed until well blended. Press dough into bottom of prepared pan. Bake 20 minutes.

3. Meanwhile, beat eggs in large bowl until fluffy and light in color. Add sugar, corn syrup, vanilla and salt; beat until well blended. Pour over crust; sprinkle evenly with pecans.

4. Bake 25 to 30 minutes or until center is just set. Cool completely in pan on wire rack. Cut into bars.   *Makes about 2 dozen bars*

Tropical Sunshine Cake

Sweetheart Chocolate Mini Bundt Cakes

1 package (18.25 ounces) yellow
    cake mix
1 can (12 fluid ounces) NESTLÉ®
    CARNATION® Evaporated
    Milk
2 large eggs
1 can (20 ounces) crushed pineapple
    in juice, drained (juice reserved),
    divided

½ cup chopped almonds
¾ cup sifted powdered sugar
1 cup flaked coconut, toasted
    Whipped cream

PREHEAT oven to 350°F. Grease 13×9-inch baking pan.

COMBINE cake mix, evaporated milk and eggs in large mixer bowl. Beat on low speed for 2 minutes. Stir in *1 cup* pineapple. Pour batter into prepared baking pan. Sprinkle with almonds.

BAKE for 30 to 35 minutes or until wooden pick inserted in center comes out clean. Cool in pan on wire rack for 15 minutes.

COMBINE sugar and 2 tablespoons *reserved* pineapple juice in small bowl; mix until smooth. Spread over warm cake; sprinkle with coconut and *remaining* pineapple. Cool completely before serving. Top with whipped cream.   *Makes 12 servings*

1⅔ cups all-purpose flour
½ cup unsweetened cocoa powder
1 teaspoon baking soda
¼ teaspoon salt
1 cup plus 2 tablespoons buttermilk
¾ cup packed brown sugar

¾ cup mayonnaise
1 teaspoon vanilla
1 cup semisweet chocolate chips,
    divided
¼ cup whipping cream

1. Preheat oven to 350°F. Spray 6 mini bundt pans with nonstick cooking spray.

2. Combine flour, cocoa, baking soda and salt in medium bowl. Beat buttermilk, brown sugar, mayonnaise and vanilla in large bowl with electric mixer at medium speed until well blended. Gradually add flour mixture; beat 2 minutes or until well blended. Stir in ½ cup chocolate chips.

3. Spoon batter evenly into prepared pans. Bake 22 minutes or until toothpick inserted near centers comes out clean. Cool in pans 15 minutes; invert onto wire rack to cool completely.

4. Place remaining ½ cup chocolate chips in small bowl. Heat cream in small saucepan over low heat until bubbles form around edge of pan; pour over chips. Let stand 5 minutes; stir until smooth. Cool until slightly thickened; drizzle over cakes.

Makes 6 mini bundt cakes

Delicious Strawberry Torte

German Upside Down Cake

4 eggs, separated
1 package (about 18 ounces) yellow cake mix
1⅓ cups milk
1 package (4-serving size) vanilla instant pudding and pie filling mix
¼ cup vegetable oil
1 teaspoon vanilla
1 container (16 ounces) vanilla frosting
1 quart strawberries, stemmed and halved
Whole strawberries (optional)

1. Preheat oven to 375°F. Grease and flour two 9-inch round cake pans.

2. Beat egg whites in medium bowl with electric mixer at high speed until soft peaks form. Beat cake mix, milk, pudding mix, egg yolks, oil and vanilla in large bowl at medium speed 2 minutes or until until well blended. Fold in egg whites. Pour batter into prepared pans.

3. Bake 28 to 32 minutes or until toothpick inserted into centers comes out clean. Cool in pans 15 minutes. Remove to wire racks; cool completely.

4. Cut each cake layer in half horizontally. Place 1 layer half on serving plate. Spread with one fourth of frosting; top with one third of strawberry halves. Repeat with remaining cake layer halves, frosting and strawberry halves, ending with frosting. Garnish top with whole strawberries. *Makes 10 to 12 servings*

1½ cups shredded coconut
1 cup chopped pecans
1 container (16 ounces) coconut pecan frosting
1 package (about 18 ounces) German chocolate cake mix
1⅓ cups water
4 eggs
1 cup milk chocolate chips
⅓ cup vegetable oil
Whipped cream (optional)

1. Preheat oven to 350°F. Spray 13×9-inch glass baking dish with nonstick cooking spray.

2. Spread coconut evenly in prepared pan. Sprinkle pecans over coconut. Spoon frosting by tablespoonfuls over pecans. (Do not spread.)

3. Beat cake mix, water, eggs, chocolate chips and oil in large bowl with electric mixer at low speed 30 seconds. Beat at medium speed 2 minutes or until well blended and creamy. Pour batter into prepared pan, spreading carefully over frosting.

4. Bake 35 to 40 minutes or until toothpick inserted into center comes out clean. Cool in pan 10 minutes; invert onto serving plate. Serve warm. Top with whipped cream, if desired. *Makes 12 to 15 servings*

Pink Lady Cake

Red Velvet Cake

1 package (about 18 ounces) devil's
  food cake mix, plus ingredients
  to prepare mix
1 container (16 ounces) vanilla
  frosting

Red food coloring
1 package (3 ounces) ladyfingers,
  split in half
Pink satin ribbon (optional)

1. Preheat oven to 350°F. Grease two 8-inch round cake pans.

2. Prepare cake mix according to package directions. Pour batter into prepared pans. Bake 30 minutes or until toothpick inserted into centers comes out clean. Cool completely in pans on wire racks.

3. Combine frosting and enough food coloring in large bowl until desired shade of pink is reached. Remove cake layers from pans. Place one layer on serving plate; spread with frosting. Top with second cake layer; frost top and side of cake.

4. Arrange ladyfingers around side of cake, pressing flat sides into frosting as shown in photo. Tie ribbon around cake, if desired.   *Makes 10 to 12 servings*

---

2 packages (about 18 ounces each)
  white cake mix
2 teaspoons baking soda
3 cups buttermilk
4 eggs

2 bottles (1 ounce each) red food
  coloring
2 containers (16 ounces each) vanilla
  frosting

1. Preheat oven to 350°F. Grease and flour four 9-inch round cake pans.

2. Combine cake mixes and baking soda in large bowl. Add buttermilk, eggs and food coloring; beat with electric mixer at low speed until moistened. Beat at high speed 2 minutes.

3. Pour batter into prepared pans. Bake 30 to 35 minutes or until toothpick inserted into centers comes out clean. Cool in pans 10 minutes. Remove to wire racks; cool completely.

4. Place one cake layer on serving plate; spread with frosting. Repeat with second and third cake layers. Top with fourth cake layer; frost top and side of cake.

Makes 16 servings

Tres Leches Cake

Chocolate-Covered Coconut Almond Cake

1 package (about 18 ounces) white
   cake mix, plus ingredients to
   prepare mix
1 can (14 ounces) sweetened
   condensed milk

1 cup milk
1 cup whipping cream
1 container (8 ounces) whipped
   topping, thawed
Fresh fruit (optional)

1. Preheat oven to 350°F. Spray 13×9-inch baking pan with nonstick cooking spray.

2. Prepare cake mix according to package directions. Pour batter into prepared pan. Bake 35 to 40 minutes or until toothpick inserted into center comes out clean. Cool in pan 5 minutes.

3. Combine condensed milk, milk and whipping cream in 4-cup measure. Poke holes all over warm cake with wooden skewer or toothpick. Slowly pour milk mixture evenly over top of cake. Let cake stand 10 to 15 minutes to absorb liquid. Cover and refrigerate at least 1 hour.

4. When completely cool, spread whipped topping over cake. Garnish with fruit. Keep cake covered and refrigerated.   *Makes 12 to 15 servings*

¾ cup toasted sliced almonds, divided
1 package (about 18 ounces) yellow
   cake mix
1 package (4-serving size) vanilla
   instant pudding and pie
   filling mix
4 eggs
1 cup sour cream

¾ cup water
¼ cup vegetable oil
½ teaspoon vanilla
½ teaspoon coconut extract
⅔ cup shredded coconut, divided
½ cup whipping cream
½ cup semisweet chocolate chips

1. Preheat oven to 350°F. Spray 10- or 12-cup bundt pan with nonstick cooking spray. Coarsely chop ½ cup almonds.

2. Beat cake mix, pudding mix, eggs, sour cream, water, oil, vanilla and coconut extract in large bowl with electric mixer at low speed 30 seconds. Beat at medium speed 2 minutes. Fold in chopped almonds and ⅓ cup coconut. Pour batter into prepared pan. Bake 1 hour or until toothpick inserted near center comes out clean. Cool in pan 15 minutes; invert onto wire rack to cool completely.

3. Heat cream in small saucepan just until hot. (Do not boil.) Remove from heat; add chocolate chips and let stand 2 minutes. Whisk until smooth. Let stand at room temperature 15 minutes or until thickened. Stir; pour over cake. Sprinkle with remaining ¼ cup almonds and ⅓ cup coconut. Refrigerate until ready to serve.

Makes 10 to 12 servings

Apple Spice Custard Cake

Easy Lemon Cake Roll

1 (18.25-ounce) package spice
　　cake mix
2 medium apples, peeled, cored and
　　chopped
1 (14-ounce) can EAGLE BRAND®
　　Sweetened Condensed Milk
　　(NOT evaporated milk)

1 (8-ounce) container sour cream
¼ cup lemon juice
　　Ground cinnamon (optional)

1. Preheat oven to 350°F. Grease and flour 13×9-inch baking pan.

2. Prepare cake mix according to package directions. Stir in apples. Pour batter into prepared pan. Bake 30 to 35 minutes or until toothpick inserted near center comes out clean.

3. In medium bowl, combine EAGLE BRAND® and sour cream; mix well. Stir in lemon juice. Remove cake from oven; spread sour cream mixture evenly over hot cake.

4. Return to oven; bake 5 minutes or until set. Sprinkle with cinnamon (optional). Cool. Chill. Store leftovers covered in refrigerator.　　　　*Makes one (13×9-inch) cake*

Prep Time: 15 minutes
Bake Time: 35 to 40 minutes

½ cup powdered sugar
1 package (about 16 ounces) angel
　　food cake mix
1¼ cups water
1 package (4-serving size) lemon
　　instant pudding and pie
　　filling mix

2 cups cold milk
1 container (12 ounces) whipped
　　topping
2 to 3 drops yellow food coloring
　　(optional)
1½ cups shredded coconut

1. Preheat oven to 350°F. Spray 17×12-inch jelly-roll pan with nonstick cooking spray. Line with waxed paper. Sprinkle clean towel with powdered sugar.

2. Beat cake mix and water in large bowl according to package directions. Pour batter into prepared pan. Bake 17 minutes or until toothpick inserted into center comes out clean. Immediately invert cake onto prepared towel. Fold towel edge over cake and roll up cake and towel jelly-roll style. Place seam side down on wire rack to cool completely.

3. Combine pudding mix and milk in medium bowl; whisk 2 minutes or until thickened. Fold in whipped topping and food coloring, if desired. Refrigerate until ready to use.

4. Unroll cake, removing towel. Reserve 1 cup pudding; spread remaining pudding evenly onto cake. Re-roll cake; place seam side down on platter. (If cake breaks, hold pieces together and continue to roll.) Frost cake with reserved 1 cup pudding; sprinkle with coconut. Cut 1 inch off each end with serrated knife; discard scraps. Cover; refrigerate 2 to 3 hours before serving.　　　　*Makes 10 servings*

Peanut Butter & Cookie Cake

Chocolate Syrup Swirl Cake

1 package (about 18 ounces) white
    cake mix
1 package (4-serving size) vanilla
    instant pudding and pie
    filling mix
4 eggs
½ cup milk

⅓ cup vegetable oil
¼ cup water
¼ cup creamy peanut butter
2 cups chopped peanut butter
    cookies, divided
½ cup semisweet chocolate chips
1 teaspoon shortening

1. Preheat oven to 350°F. Spray 12-cup bundt pan with nonstick cooking spray.

2. Beat cake mix, pudding mix, eggs, milk, oil, water and peanut butter in large bowl with electric mixer at medium speed 2 minutes or until well blended. Stir in 1¾ cups chopped cookies. Pour batter into prepared pan.

3. Bake 50 to 60 minutes or until toothpick inserted near center comes out clean. Cool in pan 15 minutes; invert onto wire rack to cool completely.

4. Combine chocolate chips and shortening in small microwavable bowl. Microwave on HIGH 1 minute; stir. Microwave at additional 15-second intervals until melted and smooth. Spoon glaze over cake; sprinkle with remaining ¼ cup chopped cookies.

Makes 10 to 12 servings

---

1 cup (2 sticks) butter or margarine,
    softened
2 cups sugar
2 teaspoons vanilla extract
3 eggs
2¾ cups all-purpose flour

1¼ teaspoons baking soda, divided
½ teaspoon salt
1 cup buttermilk or sour milk*
1 cup HERSHEY₂S Syrup
1 cup MOUNDS® Sweetened
    Coconut Flakes (optional)

To sour milk: Use 1 tablespoon white vinegar plus milk to equal 1 cup.

1. Heat oven to 350°F. Grease and flour a 12-cup fluted tube pan or 10-inch tube pan.

2. Beat butter, sugar and vanilla in large bowl until fluffy. Add eggs; beat well. Stir together flour, 1 teaspoon baking soda and salt; add alternately with buttermilk to butter mixture, beating until well blended.

3. Measure 2 cups batter in small bowl; stir in syrup and remaining ¼ teaspoon baking soda. Add coconut, if desired, to remaining vanilla batter; pour into prepared pan. Pour chocolate batter over vanilla batter in pan; do not mix.

4. Bake 60 to 70 minutes or until wooden pick inserted in center comes out clean. Cool 15 minutes; remove from pan to wire rack. Cool completely; glaze or frost as desired.

Makes 20 servings

Carrot Cake Cookies

Extra Chunky Peanut Butter Cookies

1½ cups all-purpose flour
1 teaspoon ground cinnamon
½ teaspoon baking soda
½ teaspoon salt
¾ cup packed brown sugar
½ cup (1 stick) butter, softened
1 egg

½ teaspoon vanilla
1 cup grated carrots (about
   2 medium)
½ cup chopped walnuts
½ cup raisins or chopped dried
   pineapple (optional)

1. Preheat oven to 350°F. Grease cookie sheets or line with parchment paper.

2. Combine flour, cinnamon, baking soda and salt in medium bowl. Beat brown sugar and butter in large bowl with electric mixer at medium speed until creamy. Add egg and vanilla; beat until well blended. Beat in flour mixture. Stir in carrots, walnuts and raisins, if desired. Drop dough by rounded tablespoonfuls 2 inches apart onto prepared cookie sheets.

3. Bake 12 to 14 minutes or until set and edges are lightly browned. Cool on cookie sheets 1 minute. Remove to wire racks; cool completely.

Makes about 3 dozen cookies

---

2 cups all-purpose flour
1 teaspoon baking soda
½ teaspoon salt
1 cup chunky peanut butter
¾ cup granulated sugar
½ cup packed light brown sugar
½ cup (1 stick) butter, softened

2 eggs
1 teaspoon vanilla
1½ cups chopped chocolate-covered
   peanut butter cups (12 to
   14 candies)
1 cup dry roasted peanuts

1. Preheat oven to 350°F. Line cookie sheets with parchment paper or lightly grease.

2. Combine flour, baking soda and salt in medium bowl. Beat peanut butter, granulated sugar, brown sugar and butter in large bowl with electric mixer at medium speed until creamy. Beat in eggs and vanilla. Add flour mixture; beat until well blended. Stir in chopped candy and peanuts. Drop dough by rounded tablespoonfuls 2 inches apart on prepared cookie sheets.

3. Bake 13 minutes or until set. Cool on cookie sheets 1 minute. Remove to wire racks; cool completely.

Makes about 4 dozen cookies

Chocolate Strawberry Stackers

Citrus Coolers

2½ cups powdered sugar, divided
1 cup (2 sticks) plus 6 tablespoons unsalted butter, softened, divided
2 tablespoons packed light brown sugar
½ teaspoon salt, divided

2 cups all-purpose flour
½ cup semisweet chocolate chips, melted
⅓ cup strawberry jam
½ teaspoon vanilla
1 to 2 tablespoons milk (optional)

1. Beat ½ cup powdered sugar, 1 cup butter, brown sugar and ¼ teaspoon salt in large bowl with electric mixer at medium speed 2 minutes or until light and fluffy. Gradually add flour, beating well after each addition. Beat in melted chocolate until well blended. Shape dough into 14-inch log. Wrap in plastic wrap; refrigerate 1 hour.

2. Preheat oven to 300°F. Cut log into ⅓-inch-thick slices; place on ungreased cookie sheets. Bake 15 to 18 minutes or until set. Cool on cookie sheets 5 minutes. Remove to wire racks; cool completely.

3. Beat remaining 6 tablespoons butter in large bowl with electric mixer at medium speed until smooth. Beat in jam, vanilla and remaining ¼ teaspoon salt until blended. Gradually add remaining 2 cups powdered sugar; beat until fluffy. If mixture is too thick, gradually beat in milk until desired spreading consistency is reached. Spread frosting over flat sides of half of cookies; top with remaining cookies.

Makes about 20 sandwich cookies

1½ cups powdered sugar
1 package (about 18 ounces) lemon cake mix
1 cup (4 ounces) pecan pieces

½ cup all-purpose flour
½ cup (1 stick) butter, melted
Grated peel and juice of 1 large orange

1. Preheat oven to 375°F. Line cookie sheets with parchment paper. Place powdered sugar in medium bowl; set aside.

2. Beat cake mix, pecans, flour, butter, orange peel and juice in large bowl with electric mixer at medium speed until well blended. Drop dough by rounded tablespoonfuls 2 inches apart onto prepared cookie sheets.

3. Bake 13 to 15 minutes or until bottoms are light golden brown. Cool on cookie sheets 3 minutes; roll in powdered sugar. Remove to wire racks; cool completely.

Makes about 4½ dozen cookies

Prep Time: 10 minutes
Bake Time: 13 to 15 minutes

Caramel-Kissed Pecan Cookies

Waikiki Cookies

1 package (18 ounces) refrigerated
　　sugar cookie dough
½ cup all-purpose flour
1 package (2 ounces) ground pecans
12 caramel-filled milk chocolate kiss
　　candies, unwrapped

1 package (2 ounces) pecan chips
Caramel ice cream topping
　　(optional)

1. Preheat oven to 350°F. Line cookie sheet with parchment paper. Let dough stand at room temperature 15 minutes.

2. Beat cookie dough, flour and ground pecans in medium bowl with electric mixer at medium speed until well blended. Divide into 12 equal pieces. Place one candy in center of each piece of dough. Shape dough into ball around candies; seal well. Roll each ball in pecan chips. Place 2 inches apart on cookie sheet.

3. Bake 16 to 18 minutes or until light golden around edges. Cool on cookie sheet 2 minutes.

4. If desired, warm caramel topping according to package directions. Drizzle over warm cookies. Remove to wire rack; cool completely. Store in airtight container.

Makes 1 dozen cookies

1½ cups packed light brown sugar
⅔ cup shortening
1 tablespoon water
1 teaspoon vanilla
2 eggs
1¾ cups all-purpose flour

½ teaspoon salt
¼ teaspoon baking soda
1 cup white chocolate chunks
1 cup macadamia nuts, coarsely
　　chopped

1. Preheat oven to 375°F.

2. Beat brown sugar, shortening, water and vanilla in large bowl with electric mixer at medium speed until well blended. Add eggs; beat well.

3. Combine flour, salt and baking soda in medium bowl. Add to sugar mixture; beat at low speed just until blended. Stir in white chocolate chunks and nuts.

4. Drop dough by rounded tablespoonfuls 2 inches apart onto ungreased cookie sheets.

5. Bake 7 to 9 minutes or until set. (Do not overbake.) Cool on cookie sheets 2 minutes. Remove to wire racks; cool completely.

Makes about 3 dozen cookies

Chocolate Chunk Cookies

Gingery Oat and Molasses Cookies

1⅔ cups all-purpose flour
⅓ cup CREAM OF WHEAT®
    Hot Cereal (Instant, 1-minute,
    2½-minute or 10-minute cook
    time), uncooked
½ teaspoon baking soda
¼ teaspoon salt

¾ cup (1½ sticks) butter, softened
½ cup packed brown sugar
⅓ cup granulated sugar
1 egg
1 teaspoon vanilla extract
1 (11.5-ounce) bag chocolate chunks
1 cup chopped pecans

1. Preheat oven to 375°F. Lightly grease cookie sheets. Blend flour, Cream of Wheat, baking soda and salt in medium bowl; set aside.

2. Beat butter and sugars in large bowl with electric mixer at medium speed until creamy. Add egg and vanilla. Beat until fluffy. Reduce speed to low. Add Cream of Wheat mixture; mix well. Stir in chocolate chunks and pecans.

3. Drop by tablespoonfuls onto prepared cookie sheets. Bake 9 to 11 minutes or until golden brown. Let stand on cookie sheets 1 minute before transferring to wire racks to cool completely.   *Makes 24 cookies*

Tip: For a colorful item to take to school bake sales or give as a gift, replace the chocolate chunks with multicolored candy-coated chocolate.

---

1 cup all-purpose flour
¾ cup whole wheat flour
½ cup uncooked old-fashioned oats
1½ teaspoons baking powder
1½ teaspoons ground ginger
1 teaspoon baking soda
½ teaspoon ground cinnamon
¼ teaspoon salt

¾ cup sugar
½ cup (1 stick) unsalted butter,
    softened
1 egg
¼ cup molasses
¼ teaspoon vanilla
1 cup chopped crystallized ginger
½ cup chopped walnuts

1. Combine all-purpose flour, whole wheat flour, oats, baking powder, ground ginger, baking soda, cinnamon and salt in large bowl.

2. Beat sugar and butter in large bowl with electric mixer at high speed until light and fluffy. Beat in egg, molasses and vanilla. Gradually beat in flour mixture. Stir in crystallized ginger and walnuts. Shape into 2 logs about 8 to 10 inches long. Wrap in plastic wrap and chill 1 to 3 hours.

3. Preheat oven to 350°F. Grease cookie sheets. Cut logs into ⅓-inch slices. Place 1½ inches apart on prepared cookie sheets. Bake 12 to 14 minutes or until set and browned at edges. Cool on cookie sheets 5 minutes. Remove to wire racks; cool completely.   *Makes about 4 dozen cookies*

Pumpkin Chocolate Chip Sandwiches

Publications International, Ltd.   2009 Publications International, Ltd.   Recipe © 2009 Publications International, Ltd.

Holiday Treasure Cookies

1 cup solid-pack pumpkin
1 package (18 ounces) refrigerated
    chocolate chip cookie dough

¾ cup all-purpose flour
½ teaspoon pumpkin pie spice*
½ cup prepared cream cheese frosting

*You may substitute ¼ teaspoon ground cinnamon, ⅛ teaspoon ground ginger and pinch each ground allspice and ground nutmeg for ½ teaspoon pumpkin pie spice.

1. Line colander with paper towel. Place pumpkin in colander; drain about 20 minutes to remove excess moisture.

2. Preheat oven to 350°F. Grease cookie sheets. Let dough stand at room temperature 15 minutes.

3. Beat dough, pumpkin, flour and pumpkin pie spice in large bowl with electric mixer at medium speed until well blended.

4. Drop dough by rounded teaspoonfuls 2 inches apart onto prepared cookie sheets. Bake 9 to 11 minutes or until set. Cool on cookie sheets 3 minutes. Remove to wire racks; cool completely.

5. Spread about 1 teaspoon frosting on flat side of one cookie; top with second cookie. Repeat with remaining frosting and cookies.   *Makes about 2 dozen sandwich cookies*

1½ cups graham cracker crumbs
½ cup all-purpose flour
2 teaspoons baking powder
1 (14-ounce) can EAGLE BRAND®
    Sweetened Condensed Milk
    (NOT evaporated milk)
½ cup (1 stick) butter or margarine,
    softened

1⅓ cups flaked coconut
1¾ cups (10 ounces) mini kisses,
    milk chocolate or semisweet
    chocolate baking pieces
1 cup red and green holiday
    baking bits

1. Preheat oven to 375°F. In medium bowl, combine graham cracker crumbs, flour and baking powder; set aside.

2. Beat EAGLE BRAND® and butter until smooth; add reserved crumb mixture, mixing well. Stir in coconut, chocolate pieces and holiday baking bits. Drop by rounded teaspoonfuls onto greased cookie sheets.

3. Bake 7 to 9 minutes or until lightly browned. Cool 1 minute; transfer from cookie sheet to wire rack. Cool completely. Store leftovers tightly covered at room temperature.
                                                    Makes about 5½ dozen cookies

Prep Time: 10 minutes
Bake Time: 7 to 9 minutes

Cinnamon Raisin Delights

Malted Milk Cookies

1¼ cups all-purpose flour
1 teaspoon ground cinnamon
½ teaspoon salt
½ teaspoon baking soda
½ cup (1 stick) butter, softened
½ cup packed light brown sugar

¼ cup granulated sugar
1 egg, lightly beaten
1 teaspoon vanilla
1 cup raisins
¾ cup prepared vanilla frosting

1. Preheat oven to 350°F. Lightly grease cookie sheets.

2. Combine flour, cinnamon, salt and baking soda in medium bowl. Beat butter, brown sugar and granulated sugar in large bowl with electric mixer at medium speed until light and fluffy. Add egg and vanilla; beat until well blended. Add flour mixture; beat just until blended. Stir in raisins.

3. Shape dough by rounded tablespoonfuls into balls; place 2 inches apart on prepared cookie sheets.

4. Bake 11 to 13 minutes or until edges are lightly browned. Cool on cookie sheets 2 minutes. Remove to wire racks; cool completely.

5. Spread 1 tablespoon frosting on flat side of one cookie; top with second cookie. Repeat with remaining cookies and frosting.   *Makes about 1 dozen sandwich cookies*

---

1 cup (2 sticks) butter, softened
¾ cup granulated sugar
¾ cup packed light brown sugar
1 teaspoon baking soda
2 eggs
2 squares (1 ounce each)
    unsweetened chocolate, melted
    and cooled to room temperature

1 teaspoon vanilla
2¼ cups all-purpose flour
½ cup malted milk powder
1 cup chopped malted milk balls

1. Preheat oven to 375°F.

2. Beat butter in large bowl with electric mixer at medium speed until creamy. Add granulated sugar, brown sugar and baking soda; beat until blended. Add eggs, chocolate and vanilla; beat until well blended. Beat in flour and malted milk powder until blended. Stir in malted milk balls. Drop dough by rounded tablespoonfuls 2½ inches apart onto ungreased cookie sheets.

3. Bake 10 minutes or until edges are set. Cool on cookie sheets 1 minute. Remove to wire racks; cool completely.   *Makes about 3 dozen cookies*